Roger ~ ?
with a

Quixote in a Cart

James

James Nash

Matador
9 Priory Business Park,
Wistow Road, Kibworth Beauchamp,
Leicestershire. LE8 0RX
Tel: 0116 279 2299
Email: books@troubador.co.uk
Web: www.troubador.co.uk/matador
Twitter: @matadorbooks

ISBN 978 1788038 584

British Library Cataloguing in Publication Data.
A catalogue record for this book is available from the British Library.

Printed on FSC accredited paper
Printed and bound in Great Britain by 4edge Limited
Typeset in 11pt Aldine by Troubador Publishing Ltd, Leicester, UK

Matador is an imprint of Troubador Publishing Ltd

To the staff and patients of the
St John of Jerusalem Eye Hospital

Contents

Introduction

Origins

The idea came to me on a very uninspired package tour of Turkey. What was I doing sitting in a bus with a not particularly congenial load of other tourists, when in front of me lay the site of a last great adventure? I was middle-aged, divorced and my children had finished their education, so why not buy a horse and ride to Jerusalem?

Half of my life has been inextricably tangled up with the Middle East, where crusading echoes have kept intruding and surprising me; the region's history seemed to jump up like a jack-in-a-box from behind each hill, and has fascinated me for forty years.

It all began with an earlier whim. Discontented with working in my family business, a paper mill, in the mid-1950s, I decided in the middle of one night to walk from Venice to Addis Ababa. There was no logic underlying the route, no reasoning, just that I had friends in both places, and it sounded interesting and different, a good terminal point for an adventure. But in the course of that journey I caught the Arabian bug, that incurable and destructive disease, a romantic and passionate interest in things Arab which leads only and inevitably to disillusion in middle age. But then all romanticism probably meets the same end; whether you expend your passions on tribal Arabia or Irish handicrafts is irrelevant. To all romantics, middle age and disappointment will come hand in hand.

Within a couple of years, this Arabian addiction had taken me to South Yemen, as a political officer in the Colonial Service, where for six years I lived in, administered from and fought out of castles in the mountainous hinterland of Aden, a lifestyle not dissimilar to that of the crusaders settled in the Holy Land. The Colonial Office had sent me on a short Arabic course at Middle East Centre for Arabic Studies (MECAS) but I learned most of my Arabic as a child does, not from books, but from the need to communicate with the people around me – tribesmen with no word of any other language, on whom I depended and whose thoughts, ambitions and intrigues I needed to understand. The living conditions were always hard, the climate unrelenting and the landscape magnificent but brutal. The people, however, were both an endless delight and endless frustration, turbulent, entertaining and totally anarchic. I learned my trade, largely, from an Arab assistant who spoke no English, whom I addressed as 'Father' and who would reply, 'My son'. I grew totally absorbed in the lives of the little states that I tried to advise or administer. I knew each tribe, each family – I even knew most of the rebels, in the bad times, personally, so that when that particular rebellion came to an end, we would sit together around a feast of a sheep and discuss the battles in which we had been shooting at each other the month before, with laughter and light-heartedness, surprisingly devoid of malice or recriminations.

But the wars and alarms of wars were only part of it, although they became my particular forte and intensified with the increasing political pressures of the early 1960s. In the earlier years, most time was spent in trying to order the expenditure of the little state treasuries; to beg money from the Aden government to build a road, a new school or a clinic; or to start agricultural loan schemes for the purchase of pumps. The excitement and pride when the school or irrigation scheme was built was tremendous. What other job in all the world could give such rewards, such variety and such intense satisfaction, when a young man's role covered everything from planning town drains to raising his own private army? The end was bitter, bloody and full of disillusion, but friends remained, and still do.

It was there that I first heard of the St John Eye Hospital in Jerusalem, for it was famous for its research into trachoma, a major scourge in the upland states bordering the desert. Returning finally to England, via Beirut, in 1965, I found myself sitting next to an elderly gentleman in the aeroplane who was writing notes on St John writing paper.

'Excuse me, but I saw the St John emblem on your paper and I am interested in the hospital. Could you, perhaps, tell me more about it?' I asked.

'I think I can. I am the lord prior.'

The response was somewhat daunting, but we talked for the next half an hour about the hospital, the descendant of the original Knights Hospitaller hospital or hospice that was situated there in the twelfth and thirteenth centuries. It is one of the two charitable foundations of the British Order of St John, the other being the St John Ambulance.

'I don't know if there is anything that I can do, but if there is, I would like to help,' I said.

His response was to tell me to go and see the secretary-general. I did, and two years later was invited to become the esquire to the Hospitaller, then Sir Stewart Duke-Elder, the doyen of eye surgeons, who had been responsible for the rebuilding of the hospital after it had been destroyed in the battles for Jerusalem when the state of Israel was founded.

In spite of leaving Aden, Arabia would not leave me alone and I was back in the Gulf with the Foreign Office a year later, a role that neither the Foreign Office nor I found satisfactory, so again I returned home and became a chartered surveyor in the City. But still the ties held and drew me back once more. When Egypt opened its doors to foreign investment after the death of Nasser, I was the only Arabic-speaking chartered surveyor and was asked to set up an office in Cairo in 1974. I had some initial qualms, as I had been blacklisted by the Egyptians and personally abused on Cairo radio for my role in countering the Egyptian-led terrorist campaign in South Yemen, in the last few years before independence.

But times had changed and I found myself living in a crumbling villa at the foot of the pyramids, sharing an office with the man who had commanded the Egyptian air force in North Yemen. We became firm friends. We would joke about our one-time enmity on opposite sides of that war, pushing inkpots and pens around the desk to illustrate locations and strategy, like two old Colonel Blimps. The villa I had taken over from a friend from my Aden days, now a diplomat, who handed it over on leaving Cairo, complete with three cats, two dogs, a fine Arab stallion and twelve people living in the garage at the bottom of the garden. The stallion was the only horse I had ever owned purely for pleasure and exercise. Before that, horses, when I had had them, had been solely a means of transport.

It was from Cairo that I began to pursue an old dream of visiting the crusader castles. It had always been one of those *Wouldn't it be fun to…* ideas that never actually come to anything, until I discovered that the St John Museum had no photographic record of them, which gave the idea an object. So I bought a camera and a book on photography, and in the subsequent five years I travelled, in spare moments, to as many of the castles as I could reach in Syria, Jordan and southern Turkey. Thus my latest whim, however absurd, had a certain logic of its own. I had seen and done the other crusading things, but this was an aspect as yet unexperienced: the crusading journey.

Why should one not, in middle age, break loose from one's shackles and seek, in a last extravagant fling, the excitement of youth? But the shackles include conscience, which frowns on self-indulgence. Journeys must have an objective; they must start somewhere for a definable reason, end at a comprehensible and logical point, and add to the store of things. In 1097, the Crusaders had that. Between sixty thousand and a hundred thousand people, from all over Western Europe, gathered at Constantinople and from there set out to save the Eastern Church and recover the Holy Land for Christianity. Conscience, to our different way of thinking, was not over-evident in their motives, but zeal was: they mixed courage with self-sacrifice, ignorance and bigotry with faith; whole families sold or mortgaged their estates to arm and equip a son, a father or a brother, with little expectation of reward.

Their other motives were simpler – land-hunger, a lust for adventure, the loot of war, all with the approval of the Church and its indulgences to protect the participants' immortal souls. So they came, in response to the papal call, from Flanders and Normandy, from Toulouse, Lorraine and southern Italy. Thus it seemed logical to start where they had all foregathered and to follow their route to Jerusalem as nearly as modern politics would allow.

The objective followed as easily as the route. The hospital fights its way through a multitude of political and financial problems and remains, perhaps, the best-run eye hospital in the Middle East. So I approached the Order to see if my whim could be converted into something more useful by raising funds for it.

So there was the dream, the intent, but the practicalities were different. I am no horseman. Although I have ridden, on and off, since my childhood, there had always been someone else to look after the horses, to bring them to the front door and take them away afterwards. Except for once, in Ethiopia, thirty-odd years ago, when I had no front door and slept on mountainsides or in villages, but even then, there was a long-suffering and loyal groom who travelled with me and tended my mules. We travelled some four hundred miles in a month and, poor fellow, while I rode, he walked. But I had considered that my time of extravagant rushes of blood to the head and the consequent disastrous journeys was, in my middle fifties, a thing of the past. I had not ridden at all for twelve years, not since Cairo. Adventures had diminished into occasional holidays, with children, in various easily accessible and undemanding parts of Europe where the greatest hazard was the unreliable time schedules of charter flights. For years, I had done little more strenuous or risky than gardening.

Thus, I needed to get fit, to learn about horses, about which I knew little or nothing and, more specifically, to find out about horses in Turkey. The first task took a year. I started by riding trekking ponies around the Welsh hills, where I fell off and broke a rib. Next, I decided to try jumping in Kent, to get used to the unexpected – and here I fell off and broke a wrist. Then the Household Cavalry came to my rescue and under expert tuition in Knightsbridge and Hyde Park, I still fell off, but damaged nothing more serious than my ego.

In the meantime, I read all I could find on riding in Turkey, which came down to two books: Frederick Burnaby's *On Horseback Through Asia Minor*, written in the 1870s; and Christina Dodwell's *A Traveller on*

Horseback: In Eastern Turkey and Iran (1987), which had just come out. At least Christina was alive and available to question, so I invited her to dinner. That intrepid and entertaining lady had had endless problems, but not directly connected with her horses. Her Turkish ponies had served her well.

'You will find a couple of hay nets useful, and take some anti-fly mixture for your horses,' she advised. I acquired both. The anti-fly mixture I could well have used, but I managed to lose it somewhere along the route before the weather got hot enough to make it necessary, and the hay nets would not retain the chopped straw which in Turkey replaces hay. I gave them away.

The redoubtable Captain Burnaby's horses caused no problems either. A big man, well over six feet tall, his praise of the stamina, if not the elegance, of Turkish horses rang like a paean over the intervening century. There is a fine portrait of him in the National Portrait Gallery.

I went on a brief visit to Istanbul in June 1987, to see the chairman of the Turkish Jockey Club, whom I had met in England and who had offered to help. As we discussed the possibilities, it became clear that there were problems. Although there is a thriving racing industry in Turkey, the horse as a means of transport has all but disappeared in the last thirty years. Small ponies abound, pulling carts around most provincial towns, but riding horses capable of carrying my weight do not. The government-owned Karacabey stud, however, does breed Arab/Haflinger crosses to improve the stock of local working horses. After a few telephone calls to the stud and the Ministry of Agriculture, it was arranged that the stud would look at its books to see if it could produce and train up one or two of these crosses.

In November, I returned to Istanbul. I had booked into the Pera Palace Hotel, as it seemed an appropriate place from which to be planning a nine-hundred-year-out-of-date journey. With its 1800s rococo exterior and a mock quattrocento Mameluke interior, the hotel's sense of history seemed to be as confused as my own in pretending to be an Apulian Norman – for they too had joined the First Crusade at Constantinople. Its lift is magnificent, a silver-painted wrought-iron affair that rattles its way up and down, carrying not only the usual gaggle of tourists, one feels, but the ghosts of long-dead minor Balkan royalty, in flamboyant but slightly tarnished uniforms. I think this confused sense of history is the reason that the hotel's alarm call system does not work: the staff can never remember in which century they were meant to wake you up, so they don't bother. There was also a sentimental reason for my choice of accommodation: my father had stayed there at the end of the First World War, on his way back from South Russia. The hotel had charged him £11 for one night but, on being offered a sovereign instead, had brought him £10 change. Unfortunately, their rates were not so favourable when I visited.

I called again on the Jockey Club chairman, Özdemir Atman, to discover that the Karacabey stud was unable to help. I was still horseless. However, he arranged for me to see some thoroughbreds at a riding club on the eastern side of the city. There seemed no alternative, so, filled with misgivings and very conscious of my own lack of knowledge, I bought two of them for £1,500. The Jockey Club offered to look after them until my return in March 1988, and to try to find a groom to accompany me.

Having a day to spare before my return flight, I took a ferry to Yalova, a sentimental repeat of part of my journey from Venice to Ethiopia. Mist obscured the views of the Bosphorus and, from lack of Turkish, I sat in silence. I exchanged smiles with a wrinkled peasant lady and her Pooter-like husband, the pair clucking over each other like loving, elderly hens, and I watched a travelling salesman extolling and demonstrating his wares. It was a work of art. Juice extractors were inserted into oranges and the juice flowed freely into a glass. Patent vegetable slicers cut patterned pieces of cucumber and the pieces were flourished as if they were the finest lace, all to a patter of sales talk that produced oohs and aahs and laughter at the ingenuity. Pockets were searched for a handful of coins or small-denomination notes and a slicer changed hands, but it was a small return for the showmanship and the entertainment provided. The ferry returned to Istanbul, and I to London.

The next four months passed in a flurry of seeking sponsorship, training, and buying saddlery which, in the latter case, was complicated by a total ignorance of what was suitable. The sponsorship was simple – I wrote to everybody I knew – but for the rest, each piece of advice contradicted the last one. As the mountains of equipment grew in every corner of my small house, the only limit that I seemed to stick to was the number of books: three. How does one select books for a long journey, when weight and space are at such a premium? Nothing too easy to read, I thought, nothing connected with the journey, and preferably very English. I almost kept to this with Trollope, Milton's *Paradise Lost* and – a bit of backsliding – Herodotus' *Histories*. In the past, I had always taken Archibald Wavell's *Other Men's Flowers*, but discarded it this time, which proved a mistake. A good anthology of poetry is infinitely rereadable, and should I ever do this sort of thing again, I will not repeat the mistake.

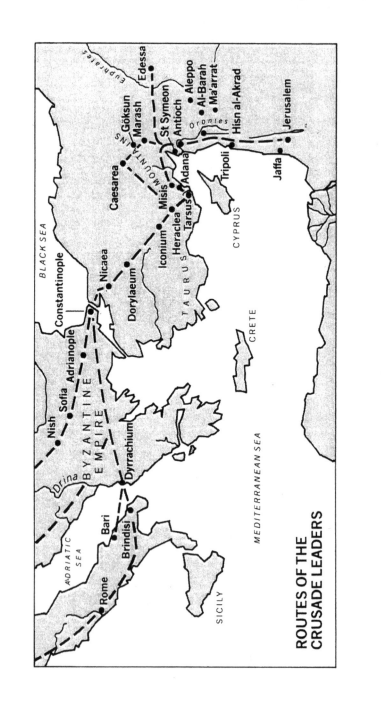

ROUTES OF THE
CRUSADE LEADERS

I

A Chapter of Accidents

Struggling under a whole Himalaya of saddlery, I flew out to Istanbul in early March 1988, sitting next to Tim Severin, the travel writer and adventurer, in the aeroplane, who had already ridden from Belgium to Bozüyük, some 150 miles south of Istanbul, following the route of Godfrey de Bouillon. He was going to look at the horses that he had left there in November and was planning to return again in May, to complete the journey along almost the same route as I had planned. He regaled me with tales of his trip so far, but I felt, with each new entertaining story, how totally inadequate my own preparations had been.

I have never been at ease in Istanbul; I associate it with loneliness. Loneliness is a feature of all large cities where one is a stranger, and even more so when one lacks the language, but for me, Istanbul is the ultimate expression of it. Perhaps it is just the moments when I have found myself there, times when the loneliness was already in me and the city had nothing to do with it, but one cannot disassociate places from emotions felt there,

1

ISTANBUL

regardless of their origins. They colour the images and shape the memories.

It has, of course, the most dramatic and romantic skylines in the world; seen from the sea or from the Golden Horn, the domes and minarets are incomparable. Yet the whole has an air of a decaying Second Empire dower house. The *grande dame* still lives there, but has fallen on hard times. The jewellery has all gone, as have the best pictures and the silver; only the dusty bric-a-brac of an unfashionable age remains. Yet in the middle of it, if one knows where to look, there are still jewels to be seen, Ottoman architectural jewels that gleam through centuries of decline.

Of the awe-inspiring city that dazed the first rude crusaders, little remains. Abetted and directed by the Venetians, the Fourth Crusade, in 1204, turned on their co-religionists and devastated the city with a savagery comparable only with that of the Mongols. Most of what survived the sack was, in its turn, swept away by the successive and uncontrollable fires that plagued Constantinople until this century.

But it would have been fascinating to see those first meetings of the crusader princes and the Byzantine Emperor Alexius, the blunt and relatively simple Westerners whose lives were devoted to the arts of war and the subtle, sophisticated emperor of a state still rich beyond the dreams of the West, but where soldiers were considered an unfortunate necessity and war not a thing of honour, but a failure of imperial policy. It is hardly surprising that the two sides rarely understood either the tactics or philosophy of their allies. The two cultures were miles apart.

3

As the Pera Palace was full, my travel agent booked me into the Yesil Ev (the Green House), a lovely restored Ottoman private house, replete with Second Empire furnishings. Every afternoon a pianist in the hotel lounge would play light classics and somewhat dated popular songs, giving the whole an air of *gemütlich* Victorianism, a little frayed around the edges. I unloaded my Himalaya of equipment from the taxi and carted the saddlery off to the racecourse stables, where the horses appeared well and the measures of whisky supplied by the general manager, Ilhan Erarslan, were more than liberal. He told me that an article in *Banko*, the Turkish equivalent of *Sporting Life*, had produced a groom, who was due to arrive in a day or so.

'Only two people contacted them,' said Ilhan, 'and one was a little mad, but this fellow we know, and is all right.'

The following morning, I went to try out the horses, to find them grossly under-exercised – they had not been ridden at all during the four months. One, Gunday, a 16.3-hand stallion, was virtually unrideable; while the other, Fayun, a 16.1-hand gelding, was in a muck sweat after half an hour of walking and shying.

That evening, as I dined with a merchant banker friend in his flat overlooking the Bosphorus, dinner was interrupted by a telephone call from Gloucestershire; his village parson had died and he owned the living.

'What about So-and-So? Would he like it? Oh, you have already spoken to him, splendid – well, let's give it to him.' I wonder when, if ever, was the last English parson appointed to his English benefice by a message from Asia?

Yusuf, the groom, arrived from Izmir. A sturdy, moustachioed, twenty-five-year-old Kurd from Tarsus, he had spent most of his working life at the Izmir racecourse. In Ilhan's office we agreed a salary of £125 per month and his keep, and then set out to buy him some breeches, boots and other necessaries for the journey.

We spent a week exercising the horses: half an hour, then an hour, an hour and a half; without saddlebags, with empty saddlebags, with half-loaded saddlebags; each day increasing the workload. The horses were reshod and spare sets of shoes made.

My spare hours I spent with a Turkish poet, correcting the English proofs of his poems that had been translated by a mutual friend in London, and in trying to sort out my Syrian visa. I had applied for the visa five months before and the negotiations now continued at the Syrian Consulate General, entirely in Arabic, which I had not spoken for ten years. To my delight, I found that I could still cope, but it was hard work. Turkish was much worse. I had been learning it in odd moments over the last few months in England and could just put a sentence together, but the process of speaking it, with incessant references to the dictionary, was painfully ponderous. I had brought a spare pocket English/Turkish dictionary which I gave to Yusuf, but he proved insufficiently literate to use it and as he always spoke without attempting to moderate his speed of speech or his vocabulary, understanding him was never to be easy.

The delay in Istanbul was becoming expensive, and although I had doubts about the horses' preparedness,

YUSUF

it was time to start, however slowly, even if there was to be much more walking than riding. The prospects of physical hassles on the road appeared more attractive than the frustrations of Istanbul, even if they should prove less so when the time came and the Jockey Club laid on a horsebox to take us over the Bosphorus Bridge. On the eve of my departure, I was struck down with sultan's revenge and thought that a start in the morning would be impossible but, by dawn, things were better.

Ilhan came to see me off, pressing another packet of the best Turkish cigarettes into my hand. His kindness had been unlimited; not a horseman, but an administrator, with a command of English as poor as my Turkish, he had nevertheless guided me through endless difficulties with both people and equipment. The horsebox did not stop on the far side of the bridge, and every time I remonstrated, excuses were made – no room to turn, no room to unload – until we reached the village of Polonezköy, some ten miles on.

The village is unique. In the middle of the nineteenth century, a number of Polish refugees fled to Turkey and enrolled in the Ottoman army. For their services in the Crimean War, they were given refuge and land on the hills just south of the Bosphorus, where they built a village and a church and have retained their language and customs until today. Unlike Turkish villages, which crowd round the central mosque or market area, the Polish houses are spread out on their farms and it is the only place in Muslim Turkey to specialise in growing pigs. For an hour or two we rode and walked the horses around the scrub-covered and winter-bare

POLONEZKOY
WINDMILL

countryside showing the very first signs of blossom and mauve primulas at the roadside. We stabled the horses in the cold and empty stables of the local grandee, whose groom was the only inhabitant of the house, and found beds for ourselves in a farm that offered accommodation en pension. There was neither hay nor barley in the village, but the village taxi found some for us in the next one, a couple of miles away.

The pension's pleasant living room was decorated with three generations of family photographs, an antique clock and a stuffed pintail duck, and was warmed by a huge wood-burning stove made from an oil drum. While eating our excellent and copious supper, I explained to the mother of the house the object of my journey, with her pretty English-speaking daughter as interpreter.

'Are you a lord?' she asked.

I thought that the travelling English milord had vanished a hundred years ago, and was sorry to disappoint her.

The morning brought a sharp frost and as the only water supply was an outside, ice-cold tap, shaving was painful. In the stable, we found that Gunday had a slightly swollen leg from a cut incurred when he had been loaded in the horsebox, and Fayun had already lost a nail from a shoe. A search for the iodine took ages as the saddlebags were badly organised, and the village taxi came into use again to bring in the nearest blacksmith from ten miles away who, with great caution, dealt with the offending nail.

The blacksmithing had delayed us by a day, but we set off, after another hard frost, through pine forests to the next village, Alemdağ, a short first stage of ten miles. Firebreaks between the trees opened brilliantly lit views as we walked and rode in the sparkling sunlight. After a couple of hours, I dropped Gunday's reins for a moment as I walked, to adjust the buckle of my chaps. Gunday bolted, followed by Yusuf on foot. It was the last I was to see of either of them until the evening. I mounted Fayun in pursuit, but after a fruitless hour and a half without a sign of them, I started back on the track to Alemdağ to seek help. The gendarmerie there were as unhelpful as possible, as a self-important sergeant major continued to drill his small section of gendarmes for half an hour without deigning to speak to me and when he did, offered no help at all. I abandoned the attempt and went off to find some stabling for Fayun. A farmer with a little French offered me space in a shed crowded with farm implements – not very satisfactory, but at least a roof over Fayun's head, which I accepted gratefully and started to make enquiries about fodder.

Then, out of nowhere, Yusuf appeared. Gunday was back at Polonezköy and the contents of his saddlebags collected from all over the mountainside. However, Yusuf and the Polonezköy taxi driver, who had ferried him up and down the forest tracks, had spent most of the day under arrest. In their search, they had blundered into a military area and only a telephone call to the Jockey Club had established their bona fides. We returned to Polonezköy, where the grandee's stableman was away, so we put Gunday into the pension's cowshed for the night. With one horse here and one there, progress had been minimal, but emotions had ranged from elation

GUNDAY BOLTS!

to despair. Yusuf, after several hours chasing round the forest and as long in a military guardroom, was exhausted, and I was little better. Taking off my very dirty sock, I found my toes had turned purple where Fayun had trodden on them, and somewhere in the day's hassles, I had lost my lovely old Rolleiflex camera and Fayun had cast a shoe.

In the morning, I taxied to Alemdağ with the saddlebags, leaving Yusuf to follow on Gunday by a new and shorter route. After I had groomed Fayun in the warm sun and let him graze on the sparse grass for an hour or so, a very voluble and frightened Yusuf arrived. His flood of conversation was incomprehensible, but it emerged that Gunday had thrown him three times and he refused to ride him any further. Gunday and traffic did not seem to mix. We led a shoeless Fayun and an intractable Gunday through the fields to Resadiye, the next village, in the hope of better stabling. The village headman, or *muhtar*, and most of the menfolk were still at work in the surrounding forests, so we tethered the horses in a field and sprawled on the grass beside them until the foresters returned.

The *muhtar* in a Turkish village is an elected post with a tenure of five years. The villagers appoint one of their number who, for his period of office, acts as the village administrator, but his actual power seems to depend more on persuasion than on decree. I was to seek them out in most of the villages I passed through when in search of stabling, but although it is a position of some prestige, I was to hear many complaints about the burden of responsibility. Busy men felt it a duty to do their stint, but were pleased when their period came to an end. The Resadiye *muhtar* quickly allotted me a stable on his return; but two days out and one horse down, I was faced with selling an unrideable horse in a strange country whose language I could not speak. Half an hour's bus ride took us to Üsküdar, just across the Bosphorus from Istanbul, and a cheap hotel, two rooms for £5 sterling per night.

We were back at the stable early but ran into immediate difficulties with blacksmiths, for the blacksmith who had dealt with Fayun the day before refused to come again. He was used to shoeing donkeys and small ponies only and was much too frightened to try his skills on a racehorse so, as there was no other in the vicinity, I concentrated on disposing of the wayward Gunday. I rang Ilhan Erarslan at the Jockey Club, who said that if we sent him to the racecourse at Bursa, the manager would arrange the sale. We hired a lorry and converted it into a temporary horsebox, with bits of timber from the local timber yard built into a frame and a tarpaulin stretched over all as a canopy.

As Yusuf disappeared with the horse and lorry, I considered the cost: selling a horse seemed almost as expensive as buying one, for the bill for the afternoon's business had amounted to £100. I returned to Üsküdar, where a shave at the barber's revived flagging spirits, and after a drink with my merchant banker friend, retired to bed in the dosshouse hotel. It stank, and the single bare bulb in my airless room was only 25 watts and impossible to read by.

Frustration piled on frustration – I could still find

no blacksmith, there was still no response from the Syrians on my visa and Yusuf had vanished into thin air. I went to the stable at Resadiye with a couple of kilos of oranges for the owner's family and awaited the prodigal's return. Seated on a log in the garden, I organised a catapult competition for the children with a prize of 10p. A hail of stones flew in every direction, but when one small boy emerged as the undoubted champion, I retired to the teahouse for an hour of slow, stumbling Turkish conversation with the friendly occupants before returning to the dosshouse. At least I had learned that there was a horse fair on the outskirts of Üsküdar the following day. Yusuf arrived in the evening, having taken five and a half hours to reach Bursa the night before.

The horse fair was held in a muddy building plot and produced nothing; a cold drizzle fell on sellers, a few wretched small ponies, bunched flocks of sheep, and buyers alike. It seemed to depress them all equally. I crossed the Bosphorus and went to see the man who had sold me the horses at the riding club, but he could only offer me a tired Irish nag with tendon problems, so I returned to the dosshouse to wash my stinking clothes. Back on the Üsküdar waterfront, the weather lifted slightly, producing the most extraordinary variety and shades of light over the water and across the hills of Istanbul. It was a photographer's or a painter's dream, but I was immersed in a nightmare of dud horses.

There followed nearly a week in pursuit of new horses. On Ilhan's suggestion, I left Yusuf to look after Fayun while I caught an overnight bus to the racecourse at Adana, an uncomfortable seventeen-hour journey through rain and snow. The racecourse manager lent me a Jockey Club car with a driver and I toured the mountain villages in the Taurus foothills around Kozan, once the capital of the kingdom of Lesser Armenia. Blinding rain turned the unmade mountain roads into rivers as we went from village to village, teahouse to teahouse, but there was nothing. At Kozan, even the Armenian royal castle, which perches on its crag like a vulture, had vanished into wreaths of cloud.

Those old crusader allies, the Armenians, must have been a hardy race of hillmen. They were certainly great castle-builders and masons; the area is still filled with their ruins and the Fatimid caliphs of Egypt even brought Armenian masons to Cairo to build the new city walls. The walls are there today, a boastful exhibition of their craft, with barrel-vaulted, circular staircases in square towers and square staircases in round ones, just to show that they could. The archers' galleries combined military sophistication with an understanding of the defenders' need for light and air that was unsurpassed for years. And all this when William the Conqueror had just managed to build the White Tower of the Tower of London.

But I was still without a horse. I returned to Istanbul and, guided again by the Jockey Club, Yusuf and I caught a bus to their stud outside İzmit. As we sat drinking a glass of tea, two hundred mares and their foals grazed in sunlit fields and a skein of migrating geese flew high overhead, en route for Russia. The first blossom was bursting out, the palest pink, gleaming against an azure sky.

We explained to the stud manager that we needed a new horse for Yusuf to ride and a pack pony to lighten the burden on the other two. He drove us to a nearby village, where we found an Arab ex-racehorse, Urartu, between the shafts of a cart, and a scruffy but sturdy mountain pony for a packhorse. Yusuf rode Urartu for a few minutes and quickly declared himself satisfied, so we settled into the teahouse for the negotiations. Most of the village joined in, and an endless supply of tea and good Turkish coffee was brought out onto the patio to lubricate the wits. After the necessary hesitations and argument, I agreed to pay £300 for Urartu and £150 for the pony. Behind the teahouse, orchards led up the mountainside to the forest and snow-capped peaks that divided the valley from İznik and its lake to the west. We returned to İzmit and a good hotel for the night. It had been an idyllic day in the most beautiful surroundings.

The following morning, I paid for the pack pony and, as the local blacksmith had gone off to a fair for the day, we returned to Istanbul to hunt for a pack saddle. The two-and-a-half-hour bus journey extended to four hours in heavy traffic. Storks wheeled above the dreary industrial coastline that must have been beautiful fifty years ago, and Istanbul lay under a cloud of dust and smog, which ran out as a dirty grey line across the Sea of Marmara.

Yusuf returned to İzmit in the evening, loaded with money to pay for Urartu, the blacksmith, the lorry hire and half his next month's salary, which he had asked for in advance, to help pay his brother's hospital bill. We had agreed to meet around lunchtime at Resadiye on the following day. I arrived in good time, complete with pack saddle, but the lorry and the shoeing took longer than expected, so Yusuf and the horses did not appear until six.

As the lorry drove away, a gloomy Yusuf said, 'James *amca*?' He always addressed me as '*amca*' or 'paternal uncle', a common Turkish politeness. It was to become my name in all the villages for the next few weeks.

'Yes?'

'I left my jacket in the cab of the lorry.'

'Where is the lorry from?'

'Don't know.'

'Was there money in your jacket? What about your identity card?' All Turks are required to carry identity cards.

'I've got my money, but I lost my identity card when Gunday bolted.'

There was nothing we could do about it, but feeling sorry for him, I promised to buy him a new jacket.

The next day was Easter Sunday. I arrived late at the stable after a long delay waiting for buses, to find Yusuf and Bairam, the stable owner, breathless and harassed. The pack pony, now named Kucuk (Small) for lack of a better name, had slipped his halter and run off most of the five miles to Alemdağ. We tried the pack saddle, which fitted well enough, and the girths, which did not, but we took each animal out for exercise and Bairam had found a blacksmith who had, at last, shod Fayun. Bairam charge me £100 for the horses' keep and stabling, which I thought a bit heavy, but if I had had to chase the recalcitrant Kucuk most of the way to the next village, I too would perhaps have wanted recompense. Waiting in the teahouse for the bus, we called for a backgammon board and Yusuf trounced me.

My memories of Üsküdar will always be tainted by the ghastly dosshouse. There are other perfectly reasonable hotels, but economy was a priority and so I had to endure it. That evening I walked along the waterfront, which was scented by enticing smells from food-sellers' stalls, and went into a bar for supper of beer and *sigara burek*, cigarette-shaped rolls of fila pastry filled with white cheese. Why are Turkish bars always such depressing places? The food and drink is usually rather good, but they all have a seedy appearance and disastrous decor. Perhaps it relates to some Islamic guilty conscience; purveyors of forbidden things must not appear to be too prosperous or the places too inviting. I talked bad, broken Turkish all evening and returned to the dosshouse quite light-headed after only three glasses of beer.

On Monday, Yusuf did not bother to turn up until midday, complaining about Kucuk, who had done a Houdini trick yet again in slipping his halter. He demanded a bridle for him and medicine for Urartu, who had developed a back complaint. I relied on Yusuf's judgement of horses, but had, nevertheless, been a little surprised at how quickly he had approved of Urartu. He then dropped off the saddlebags at the dosshouse and disappeared, leaving me to buy the medicine from the chemist, without adequate Turkish to explain myself.

Having acquired the bridle and the medicine, we were off again in the morning, Yusuf leading Urartu while I rode Fayun and led Kucuk. Once on the trafficky road, Kucuk dug in his heels while Fayun danced a fandango all over the road, leaving me almost suspended in mid-air between the two. For a happy moment, I had thought we were at last making progress again. Yusuf then went on strike about riding on main roads and returned to the village; whence we found another unmetalled track through the woods. Years before, he had been injured by a racehorse he was taking through traffic on a main road and the incident with Gunday had undermined his confidence, if not his certainty that he always knew the answer. However, after four hours of walking and riding through forest, we struck open, rolling hills, boggy valleys and streams full of garrulous frogs, where herons stood poised to convert those noisy talkers into lunch.

By half-past four, we reached Samandra and waited at the foot of the inevitable clichéd statue of Atatürk, the horses grazing on the occasional tuft of grass that managed to push its way through the surrounding rubble and litter, while the *muhtar* found us stabling in the cowshed of a charming old Kurdish haji, a veteran of the Korean War. As success finally crowned the warm and hazy day, our spirits rose. But there was nowhere for us to stay, so we took a taxi back to the dosshouse for the night and to collect more medicine for Urartu's back.

Disaster came again in the night, through Yusuf's pig-headedness. After our problems with Kucuk's Houdini acts, I had suggested that we hobble him in the cowshed, but Yusuf scorned the idea and merely tied him with two halters. In the course of the night, he slipped both and went on the rampage, kicking the other two and gashing Fayun's ribs and flank.

The poor haji had heard the riot in the night and had re-secured him. As I viewed the damage, he shook his head, saying, '*O picdir, pic*. He's a bastard, a bastard', and led me back to the house for a glass of tea. Yusuf had been due to come on with the medicine for Urartu's back, which had not improved, but there was no sign of him so I retired to the teahouse where I waited until the late afternoon.

Turkish village life revolves around the teahouse or *kahveci* (literally 'coffee man'), both socially and commercially. You want to buy something, then somebody in the *kahveci* will tell you where; you want a track off the road to the next village, somebody will (mis)inform you and away you go or don't, according to the reliability of the informant. Notices abound declaring that those under eighteen are not permitted, and women stay well away, for this is the Turkish village's equivalent of the English gentleman's club, before the advent of 'henhouses'. Above the low hubbub of conversation, a black-and-white television hums, showing endless old American or British films, all dubbed. I once watched a whole episode of *Yes, Prime Minister* without understanding a single word of it; the ultimate frustration. How the *kahveci* himself makes a living, I have never understood. The world, without his wife, seems to sit there all day playing cards, dominoes or backgammon, and only rarely buys his glass of corrosive, hot, sweet tea. Perhaps the *kahveci* has a cow or field out the back. That day, I consumed gallons of his tea but, as a stranger and a guest, was never allowed to pay for it.

All these delays had played havoc with my reading. I had finished Trollope, had devoured Herodotus as if it was a Dick Francis and was already down only to *Paradise Lost*. Yusuf turned up at the dosshouse at six. He had been picked up in a police round-up the night before after some incident in Istanbul and, being without an identity card, had been locked up until the early afternoon. He had then gone straight to Samandra and had seen the damage. He arrived very angry, very tired and, after I had added my bit, very depressed. I went out to friends for supper and borrowed an armful of paperbacks. We would not be going anywhere until Fayun and Urartu were fit again.

I called in a vet to look at both of them, who gave me a prescription for each and advised three or four days' rest. After daily visits to the stables, I would return to drift, aimlessly and miserably, around Istanbul. I am not a good tourist, and although I have always loved Aya Sofya and the Topkapı Palace, particularly the Chinese porcelain collection there, I could concentrate on nothing, with half my mind awaiting the next nail in this prolonged crucifixion.

The next nail was struck on the fourth day. I reached Samandra to find Fayun gone, together with a saddle and a bridle. A thief had come in the night, cut his halter, saddled him up and vanished. The poor old haji, much distressed, had heard nothing. The remainder of the day was spent at the gendarmerie headquarters at Kartal, seven miles away on the coast, but without any news. A strange conversation developed there, with the corporal in charge of the investigation, about the loss of Turkish honour in the theft and religion, but mainly about religion, for the corporal was a Sufi, a follower of Islamic mysticism. I told him that I was the only Christian he was likely to meet who had built a mosque. It had been about twenty-five years before, a very basic affair that I had built for my guards in South Yemen. I even found that, after all those intervening years, I could still remember the first sura of the Koran; it was an interesting conversational interlude, but did nothing towards finding Fayun.

The haji found him the following day, on a hillside only three or four miles away. Obviously his trick of only going backwards when frightened had defeated the thief, who had abandoned him in disgust. Apart from the loss of yet another shoe, Fayun was no worse for the experience.

We found a blacksmith who would come if we gave Fayun a tranquilising injection, so we trooped back to the vet for, in addition, Urartu's back had not improved. The vet could suggest nothing for Urartu, but the Jockey Club knew of a quack of the last resort, who some of their owners swore by for back problems. So I sought out Bobby, the quack, and another £100 changed hands. A day or so later he arrived at the stables and applied a foul-smelling concoction, with instructions on its continued application for the next three or four days. As far as I could understand with my minimal Turkish, the horrible brew lacked only the eye of a newt to match that of Macbeth's witches.

OBVIOUSLY HIS TRICK OF ONLY GOING BACKWARDS WHEN FRIGHTENED ——

The weather had turned cold and grey and I had developed a heavy cold, so I retired to the dosshouse with a decent light bulb and read five borrowed detective stories and a P. G. Wodehouse. I then found a shop with some English books in the book bazaar by the Beyazit Mosque, where I bought *The Mill on the Floss*, Bogarde's autobiography, *Persuasion* and *Emma*. I had not read any Jane Austen since my days in South Yemen, when I had sat in one of my little fortress houses and read straight through the lot.

The witches' brew proved to be as ineffectual as the vet's earlier potions, so I decided to get rid of Urartu and travel on with only the other two horses. I wished I had shot the poor beast in the beginning and cut my costs, for my vet's bill had amounted to over £150 altogether for a horse that had not worked for a single day. The arrangements took another day or so and we were off again.

We started in the middle of the morning, in heavy mist that soon turned to rain, along the course of an unfinished motorway to avoid traffic. The surface was soft and glue-like as we zigzagged in search of the firmest going. Suddenly, Fayun sank up to his belly in a quagmire. Getting off was almost impossible, and I was soon struggling beside him in the mud. I dragged myself out, but the weight of saddlebags and saddle was too much for poor Fayun, and he still could not move. I waded back in and released the saddle and bags, while Yusuf pulled at the bridle. Within a few minutes, we were both out, mud-soaked but otherwise unharmed. Yusuf was highly critical of my performance.

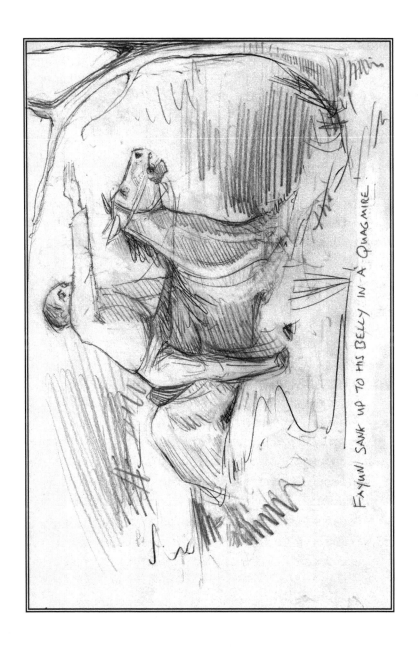

FAYUN SANK UP TO HIS BELLY IN A QUAGMIRE.

'Why didn't you follow immediately behind me?' he complained, but was quickly silenced when, two miles further on, he did exactly the same himself.

We reached a village at four o'clock, damp and bedraggled, to find good stabling, but no tea at the *kahveci*, only long faces. We had both forgotten that it was the first day of Ramadan, the fasting month. Nor could the village produce fodder or accommodation, so we took the village taxi again to find a corn chandler and then a hotel in a small town on the coast, six miles away.

The next day began with a row. Yusuf refused to carry on in the bad weather. He had heard a weather forecast on the radio, predicting snow.

'I thought,' I said, 'that I had found a hero to travel with me, but I see I merely found a goat', and I sacked him. I took a taxi to the Jockey Club stud to collect the money from the sale of Gunday, ruminating pleasurably on being able to produce satisfying insults, in spite of my poor Turkish. But on my return, we made it up.

I had chosen the mountain road from Istanbul to İzmit as the coast road was full of heavy traffic. We travelled slowly for a week, riding where we could, but walking along the unavoidable stretches of tarmac to save the horses' feet, and resting every third day. The weather was not kind and with a lot of walking in permanently wet boots, I grew a crop of painful blisters, so was as glad as the horses of the rest days. Yusuf talked incessantly and incomprehensibly, but my replies were limited to yeses, noes and grunts. Each evening we managed to find stabling at reasonable prices, but nowhere to stay and often no fodder, so the taxi bills began to mount up and cost more than either the fodder or the grubby little lorry-drivers' hotels where we stayed in the coastal towns.

When the rain stopped, it was lovely. The hills were full of grape hyacinths, St John's wort and broom. Beech and oak woods were filled with cuckoos, a pleasing reminder of Englishness; falcons burst from beneath our feet, wheeling and playing across the valleys; while the now-ubiquitous stork, in the swollen streams and gullies, shared the pursuit of the frog parliaments with the herons. A sporting farmer pointed out a scrub-covered hillside which, he said, was excellent for woodcock but, with the milder weather, they would soon be migrating to Russia. In the oak scrub, there was an occasional flare of blossom on a crab or apple tree that had translated itself into the wilderness, and in the flooded bottoms, the little green frogs chattered incessantly.

We stopped at the Jockey Club stud, a few miles beyond İzmit, for a day's rest and to refit one of Fayun's shoes. We all needed the rest: the horses had been worked hard and I was feeling ill. The blacksmith refitted the shoe on a glorious smiling morning, an ideal English spring morning, but who ever heard such an orchestra of nightingales on an English morning? The woods were full of them. But the blacksmith's skills did not match the setting; within two and a half hours, the shoe was off again, a record of bad workmanship which forced us to stop at the nearest village.

The Turkish blacksmith is a curse
Whose work is either bad or worse.

What you think is OK,
At the end of the day,
You discover is quite the reverse.

By this time, I was feeling very sick and, leaving Yusuf to feed the horses, went to İzmit in search of a doctor. It was bronchitis. I retired to bed with three packets of pills and enough disposable needles for the prescribed course of injections to make me the most banderillaed bull ever seen in a bullring. But it had been a beautiful morning.

The former glories of İzmit, ancient Nicomedia, have long disappeared (if there ever were any), ravaged by Goths, Mongols and earthquakes. There was even a tiny earthquake while I was there. It woke me in the night but did no damage. I suppose I should have been grateful for the current lack of Goths and Mongols, for I was to have quite enough problems with horses. Pliny the Younger was the governor of this Roman province of Bithynia at the end of the first century AD, and when much of İzmit was destroyed by fire, he wrote to the Emperor Trajan, recommending the establishment of a fire service.

Certainly not, came the reply, *buy 'em some buckets and tell 'em to get on with it themselves. If we start a fire service, the locals will turn it into a political trade union and cause much more trouble than the fires.*

Plus ça change, plus c'est la même chose. The crusaders too passed through it, but made no comments. Probably it was much as it is today: a prosperous small port with adequate hotels, but a dearth of good restaurants.

There remained only one disaster that had not

THERE WAS EVEN A TINY EARTHQUAKE WHILE I WAS THERE. (IZMIT)

happened, and it happened now. Yusuf again failed to secure Kucuk properly in the stable and he broke out. Yusuf pursued him, but without taking a halter as told, caught him but could not hold him, and Kucuk went under a lorry on the main road. Then Fayun, my lovely, gentle Fayun, went badly lame and the vet declared that he would be unfit to ride for months. I had never thought that a racehorse could ever be described as cuddly, but Fayun was; when I led him over terrain where I could not ride him, he would come up and nuzzle me softly from behind. I gave him away to a man with the time and facilities to keep him until he was fit again. There was nothing left but despair.

Yusuf, though depressed, was in no way contrite, nor did he accept responsibility for his part in this latest disaster. He just became more querulous, started asking for further advances of salary and became more erratic. He had begun to discover that adventures involved more than showing off in front of villagers while riding good horses, and the downside of them he did not like at all. If I had had confidence in my ability to deal with two horses alone and to find the necessary replacements myself, I would have sacked him there and then, but my Turkish was abysmal and my knowledge of horses likewise.

The search for horses began all over again. Yusuf found a small pony for his own use locally, but there was nothing big enough for me, so we took a bus to Diyarbekir, eight hundred miles away to the south-east, for twenty cramped and uncomfortable hours. Dawn brought us into the wildest mountain country and when

A CUDDLY RACEHORSE!

the bus stopped at a small town just short of Diyarbekir, we disembarked; it was near to the village of Yusuf's grandfather. Yusuf left for the village to seek advice on local horses, while I booked in at the tatty local hotel and explored the adjoining valley. The surrounding dolomite peaks and the almond- and vine-clad slopes of the valley made a splendid panorama, but I could not escape from the miseries of failure; in addition, my boots had been so warped by days of rain that they blistered my feet and were extremely painful.

Yusuf returned in the evening, with a large taxi bill. He had visited five villages without seeing a single possible horse. At the invitation of his uncle, I abandoned the hotel and returned with them to the village. Darkness had fallen and we drove up twenty-five kilometres of rough track, bouncing from rock to rock, in brilliant starlight. At one point, the driver swerved dramatically to capture four wolves in the headlights in the valley below us; surprisingly small, they did not look as if they could pose a threat to anything larger than a young lamb. In the uncle's house, discussion began about horses: the place to go was Hani, sixty kilometres away, or perhaps Dicla. There they had good horses, and large ones.

'I remember,' said one greybeard, 'horses that used to cover a hundred kilometres in a day.'

The blacksmith cousin expounded on the virtues of the local style of horseshoes, closed shoes with large studs, such as one sees in medieval manuscripts.

'They are the only ones that are any good in this sort of country,' he assured me. 'With those shoes and plenty of barley, your horses will go all day.'

The aunt, with the kindest of smiling faces, kept renewing the supplies of tea and *ayran*, a refreshing drink of slightly salted and diluted yoghurt, until supper was ready and laid on the floor in front of us.

It was decided that, in the morning, we should set off for Hani, but that I should be dropped off at some suitable point on the way and only brought in later, lest the appearance of a foreigner should raise expectations and the price.

The surrounding mountains looked bleaker at dawn than the night before had suggested until, on the lower slopes, vines softened the outlines of the barren rocks. We struggled back down the track through herds of cattle, sheep and goats to the town, where I was left to await results.

In the early afternoon, Yusuf and his friends returned. They had found something that could in no way be described as large, but appeared strong and even-tempered. We cantered it over half a mile of desert, balancing precariously on a very unstable pack saddle.

'It will carry 150 kilos,' they said, 'you will be all right with this one.'

I bought it out of necessity, not out of belief in the claims, and the deal was done at £550. I left Yusuf to get it reshod, having hired a lorry for the following day, and went on the last few miles to look at Diyarbekir.

The black basalt walls are impressive, solid and defiant. Within them little can have changed for aeons. It has an atmosphere and markets that resemble Arab towns more than Turkish, and a hundred feet below the walls, the Tigris meanders sluggishly by, a great, dull, brown snake of a river. Why do history's most famous rivers look so uninteresting? They are a terrible disappointment to the romantic imagination. But what is surprising is how much of the old town remains. Its confusing history is one of permanent bloodshed, a battered shuttlecock tossed between Romans and Sassanids, Greeks and Arabs, Arabs and Turks. It prides itself on the largest watermelons in the world, and the prize one is shown on postcards with a small boy standing inside it. It weighed a hundredweight.

The bus that returned me to İzmit was even more uncomfortable than the one that brought me. In addition, it stopped regularly at the worst roadside restaurants that it could possibly choose. Turkish buses are generally cheap, efficient and comfortable, but beware of those serving Diyarbekir! The adjoining seat contained a doting grandfather and a sick and screaming child that was waved in my face for the full twenty hours, until I tumbled out at İzmit, sleepless and dirty.

The telephone rang in my hotel room at 2.30 on the following morning, just as the Ramadan drummer began his nightly round of the town.

'Your friend and a horse are downstairs,' said the night porter. But at that hour, there was nothing that could be done, and the horse stayed in the lorry till the morning. Its journey had taken thirty-five hours.

Then Yusuf disappeared. I went to feed the horses, but only found the one Diyarbekir; the other had been moved and Yusuf had left no message. He reappeared two days later, without excuse or apologies; he just said that his brother had arrived in Istanbul.

We had planned, on the following day, to ride no farther than the next village, but there was no stable, nor at the next, or the next. We rode and walked slowly on through the foothills, back from the coast, again to avoid the traffic, along roads lined with pink and white cistus and dog roses. I rode the Diyarbekir pony, which was sprightly and eager. My old girth did not fit, causing the saddle to slip and almost ditch me in the crossing of a stream, but a spare one I had bought in Diyarbekir saved the day. The countryside rang with the song of cuckoos and nightingales, but Yusuf grumbled incessantly that his feet hurt, that we were going too far, that... But he had some justification, for we were both worried about the Diyarbekir pony after its long journey.

By mid-afternoon we at last found a stable, bedded the animals down and returned to the hotel at İzmit, where Yusuf rushed into my room late in the evening, demanding, without explanation, an immediate payment of £250, and another row ensued. I was getting very tired of that young man.

To load the horses with the saddlebags and all the paraphernalia would have been rash, so after resting them for twenty-four hours, I took the saddlebags by bus to İznik and returned to the stable by the same means. We started up the mountain in the early afternoon, a warm, muggy one that cooled as we rose to three thousand feet. As we left the farms on the lower slopes and entered the forest, our sense of direction became more and more vague, until we emerged briefly at the highest point and saw the Lake of İznik spread out below. We reorientated ourselves and sank back into a forest of enormous

My old girth did not fit!

beeches, too tall even for birdsong. The tracks led us into deep canyons, across rivers swollen by the recent rain, and up again over the next ridge. Yusuf led most of the day, swaggering with my whip and riding hat, from which he had become almost inseparable, tunelessly crooning Turkish songs.

Days later, he said that he was anxious about two or three men that he noticed trailing us through the more remote part of the mountains, but I had only seen a couple of woodcutters' children with a donkey and suspected that this vision of bandits was an attempt to boost his sense of his own heroism. Towards dusk it grew chilly and the horses were showing signs of weariness, but there was nowhere to stop. We dismounted and walked for two hours until we emerged from the forest and arrived at a village.

It was most welcoming. The *muhtar* found us some stabling and invited us to share his supper, which was brought to the *kahveci*. A crowd gathered, firing endless questions.

'Are you married?' they asked.

'No, I am divorced.'

'Will you get married again?' No Turkish villager can understand the idea of being without a wife.

'Inshallah.' (If God wills.)

'Are you a Muslim?'

'You have children?'

'Where do you live?'

The questions flowed in an endless stream, matched only by the flow of successive glasses of tea. The party continued until eleven o'clock, when the driver of the village minibus came back from the mosque to drive us to İznik and the hotel where I had left the saddlebags. But as the party spirit had been aroused, the *kahveci* stalwarts jumped into the minibus as well and the conversation continued all the thirty kilometres to the town. I slept very little that night, from the excitement of it all.

We returned early in the morning and, after a friendly farewell from the village, set out down the mountain, through a less dramatic but just as empty countryside. It soon took on the appearance of a picture-book alpine scene, with apple blossom and small green fields in the midst of scrub oak and pine-clad hillsides. But the horses were very tired and we crawled on slowly, covering under twenty kilometres in five hours before we stopped at the next village.

As we started down the mountain in yet another minibus, we were flagged down by a journalist from İznik, wanting the story and photographs, who then drove us down to the town, just in time before the bank closed for the weekend, for I was out of money. He ferried us back up the mountain with a load of fodder for the horses and down again to the hotel, where Yusuf excused himself and caught the bus into Istanbul to see his girlfriend, while I rested, worn out by the last few days and the residue of bronchitis.

II

Nicaea

The aqueduct no longer spills its flow
Of splintered light upon the cobblestones.
The gate, the squirrel-sentried walls remain
Almost, almost as I remembered them
From half a life of dreams and dreams ago,
When I walked up, exultant from the lake
Through gusting tapestries of falling snow.

The little town seemed stricken, dying, then
With gap-toothed alleys shrinking from the walls
Like last year's shrivelled walnut. Two old men
Sat silent in the teahouse, where they stared
At empty cups in which the leaves foretold
No hopeful future, nor could they recall
The gleaming panoplies of moments when

Imperial trumpets cleared the crowded street
To let the Basileus come to judge
The devious arguments of devious priests,
Whose jewelled fingers stabbed out every flaw

Within the heresies of rival sects
Whose creeds, whose faith, each sought to undermine
By dialectic or by sly deceit.

But all has changed, the aqueduct, once free,
Is channelled off to melon bed and vine,
The streets are bright with shops. The bourgeoisie
Walk down to lakeside cafes where they dine,
Or slap down *trik-trak* counters on a board
And tell old stories over sips of tea
While drawing on a bubbling *nargile*.

One feels the change, the vanished poverty,
The market throbs as if new flows of blood
Have cleansed, renewed its choking arteries;
The grey and endless visions of despair
Have lifted from the town, have disappeared,
As morning mists rise from a sun-warmed sea,
Yet still that melancholy clings to me.

I have an old affection for İznik, based on I am not sure
what – a curling black-and-white photograph of the Lefke
Gate, taken over fifty years ago and left, half-forgotten,
in a drawer; memories of youthful energy and hope, of
sunlight that caught jumbled fragments of carved stone,
abandoned, in an empty square. I remember the taste
of late-season grapes, pressed on me by a kindly lorry
driver; and small red-brown squirrels scurrying along
the top of the town walls on an unexpected warm day.
They are memories of light, infinitely variable and
bewitching light.

LEFKE GATE

I remember the snow, falling in flurries as I walked the thirty miles along the lakeside, lifting a moment, like the dancer and her veils, to reveal a slim white pencil minaret against a black backdrop, or the ruffled water of the lake and the hills beyond. A young villager who, like me, had just finished his national service, walked with me most of a day and we talked, somehow, in some inexplicable and indefinable language, of things military; a common denominator of pride. I was young, and it was magic.

Under the older name of Nicaea, it resounds through antiquity and the Middle Ages. Its early inhabitants claimed it was founded by the gods and Heracles, but poor Pliny the Younger again found its public administration was less than Olympian. They had built a theatre and a gymnasium without first surveying the site to see if the soil would bear it, which, of course, it could not.

They just forgot, they said, but like Trajan, I have my doubts about those Bithynians. Pliny, in his letters to the emperor, comes over the centuries as the archetypal treasury inspector, cautious, efficient, but always covering himself by referring back to his master. Faced with the trial of the philosopher Dio Chrysostom, from neighbouring Bursa, on a charge of peculation, he was unwilling to antagonise such a leading local figure and kept trying to pass the responsibility back to the emperor. Nor did he appear to have the instincts of a good colonial administrator. He had neither the political nose, nor the will to investigate who sold the sites to the municipality, and the tribal or family connections between vendor and purchaser. It was easier, less contentious, to say it was incompetence. But the ruins of the theatre are still there, a 1,900-year-old monument to municipal skulduggery.

But the images conjured up by the great ecumenical council, the first Council of Nicaea, in the fourth century, fill me with horror. Imagine this small if illustrious town filled with over two thousand squabbling clerics, including three hundred bishops, all arguing over the minutiae of the tenets of the Christian faith. Each faction propounded, with inflexible and pedantic passion, its own definition of the nature of Christ. Where was there for anyone to escape from it? Aubergines tainted with Arianism, Novatianism in the soup, moussaka with Monophysitism.

No wonder the Emperor Constantine told an obdurate bishop, 'Acesius, take a ladder and make your own way to Heaven!' But as they say that where there are two Greeks, there are three opinions, they probably thrived on it, at least those on the winning side of the argument; the losers finished up in exile in the more remote and unattractive corners of the empire. Perhaps the best place for peace and quiet during those frantic couple of months would have been the little hill now occupied by the tomb of Abdul Vahap; one could have sat there and stared over the town and the orchards to the lake, quite oblivious of those dialecticians tearing each other to shreds down below.

The little cathedral of Aya Sofya was not there then, the disastrous gymnasium still occupied the site, but it was to be the seat of another council, 450 years later, when they got just as excited over icons. Nowadays the

43

only clamour there is from the storks, for every spring they nest on the ruined minaret and the nestlings clatter their beaks for food, unaffected by the passing traffic or the pedantries of theological argument.

When the crusaders first came in 1097, the city had already been in Turkish hands for eighteen years; it had become the capital of the Seljuk Sultanate of Rum and was the first objective of the crusade. They reached there at the end of April when Sultan Kilij Arslan was away in Anatolia; having easily defeated the disorderly people's crusade of Peter the Hermit the previous year, the sultan did not consider that this new Western incursion was likely to cause any greater threat than its predecessor.

The siege began with the Lorrainers of Godfrey de Bouillon covering the northern side, the Apulian Normans the east and Raymond of Toulouse the southern walls. A substantial Turkish relief force attacked from the south, but after a hard-fought day, retired again to lick its wounds and leave the city to its fate, while the Crusaders cut off the heads of their slaughtered enemies and hurled them over the city walls *pour encourager les autres*.

The Seljuks, hardly a generation away from being pastoral nomads, were both physically and mentally ill-equipped for set-piece battles and sieges. A city, even their capital, was not of great moment to them. Their tradition of warfare relied on mobility and speed, the horse tribes' ability to appear out of nowhere and devastate or vanish again if the opposition was too formidable. Horses and tents still meant more to them than bricks and mortar.

The siege dragged on for another six weeks, only

becoming totally effective when the Emperor Alexius cut off supplies from the lake by hauling boats overland from the coast. When the morning planned for the final assault arrived, the crusaders awoke to find the imperial banners already flying on the walls. Alexius did not want to recover the ruins of a city whose population was largely Christian anyway, and had negotiated a Turkish surrender during the night.

The Crusaders, infuriated by the loss of loot, looked on with disgust as the leading Seljuks were led away under escort by imperial police, and they themselves were only allowed into the town in small, carefully guarded groups. However, the emperor compensated his unruly allies by presents of food to every man and a liberal distribution of the sultan's captured treasure to the princes, but distrust of the Greeks and their subtler approach to diplomacy and warfare remained and festered. Crusader bitterness is recorded in the *Gesta Francorum*, whose anonymous author describes the emperor as a fool and a knave, and believed that his charitable treatment of the prisoners was designed to injure the Franks and frustrate the crusade. So much for the charity of Western Christianity.

When I reached there, the municipal gardeners were completing new borders of petunias and installing gaudy coloured lighting along the lakeside, in preparation for the influx of holidaymakers expected for Bairam in the next few days. The whole town was busy preparing for the holiday: shops were overflowing onto pavements, counters piled high with sweets and chocolates, parents were loaded with armfuls of brightly coloured new clothes for their offspring, and only eating at conventional hours was difficult, as there remained two days of Ramadan. All I could find for breakfast was a bowl of chicken soup, rather greasy and tasteless and far from my ideal start for the day. But the weather was glorious and the place full of a profusion of roses that climbed up the second floor of houses along the main streets,

Yusuf reappeared two days later, with a damaged leg, having fallen off a motorbike to Istanbul. I doctored it as best as I could with my St John Ambulance first-aid kit and we went to look at the horses. The Diyarbekir pony was lame.

Yusuf found a buyer for the lame pony for £60, which was better than nothing, and after berating me for forcing a move from İzmit before the pony was fully rested, set off to find a replacement, while I tended and rode his mount, ferrying barley and chopped straw to the stable at Inikli by taxi. The taxi driver, who became a firm friend, would drive out to the village, from which his wife came, and wait in a teahouse by the village mosque until I had exercised the pony. The village had obviously had a period of considerable prosperity, for there were a number of substantial nineteenth-century timber-framed houses, now a little decayed, but still painted a pleasing pale blue or cream. On the road, the taxi would sometimes be forced to crawl along between the fields of vines as the ubiquitous storks were so tame that they were unwilling to move out of the way of passing traffic.

Nevertheless, in spite of the beauty of it all, the friendliness and the glorious weather, I was depressed and lethargic. My saddles were too heavy and I decided to book an air passage back to England for four or five days, to replace them with something lighter. The Bairam holiday had begun and so the airline office in Bursa was closed, but I managed to find a two-day-old *Financial Times*, the first English newspaper I had seen for weeks. On the return journey, the smart new İznik municipal bus stopped at a teahouse on the southern side of the lake, where all the passengers were given tea at the municipality's expense to celebrate the feast. I discussed pruning the olive trees with a retired sergeant major, my neighbour in the bus, but suspect I knew more about tree-pruning than he did.

Two days later, Yusuf had found, he thought, a horse that would suit, relatively nearby, and I put him in funds to complete the purchase and bring it to İznik. The airline office had reopened for business, so I took the bus again to Bursa for a ticket.

On my return to the hotel, a bedraggled little figure sat in the hotel foyer, being badgered by the town bore, the director of tourism. She was clearly both tired out and harassed by the unwanted attentions of her admirer. I extracted her from his clutches and took her around the town walls, and later to supper beside the lake. Psyche was an artist and a poet, taking a brief, lonely break from a foundering marriage. She was a delight; one moment sparkling, the next earnest, her sadness and gaiety butterfly-like in their changes. As we sat in the garden of the restaurant with our wine, we poured out our mutual loneliness and despair and talked of poetry. It was a place ordained by the gods to talk of poetry. The affinity of spirits, not unaided by the wine and the setting, turned our depressions into euphoria and we returned to the hotel arm in arm, but in the morning, I found a brief note: she had gone.

I caught the bus to Yalova and the ferry back to Istanbul. My load of saddles and saddlebags caused light-hearted banter among the other passengers.

'Who are you, John Wayne?' they joked.

As I settled down on the deck, a small voice said, 'Hello, James.' It was Psyche.

'Where are you going? Where are you staying? Why did you rush off like that without saying goodbye?'

'I don't know. I thought it was better.' She was returning to her hotel in Istanbul and there was a spare room, which I took. We dined that night in the city and as I had a day to fill before catching my plane to London, we spent it on the Bosphorus and I was bewitched, enchanted.

The few days' break in England revived my spirits and I returned with an old army trooper's saddle, to find that the ghastly Yusuf had failed to complete the deal on the horse he had talked about. Instead he had brought another all the way from Izmir at twice the price, a miserable jade, too small and much too expensive. He was also suffering from a bad earache, and with no ENT doctor locally, I sent him back to Istanbul to see one there.

For a week, I exercised two horses, riding each for an hour or so every day in the surrounding hills and the orchards around the town. As I passed, farmers would fill my pockets with cherries or load me up with small bales of fresh-cut hay, which I would try, not always successfully, to balance on the pommel of my saddle back to the stable. It was getting warmer, so I would ride one pony in the early morning and the other in the late afternoon, when Haji Ibrahim, the taxi driver, would knock on my hotel-room door to take me to Inikli. After the ride, we would sit drinking tea in the teahouse or *kahveci* for half an hour before returning, chatting with the villagers. Ibrahim was always good company; a large man for a Turk, in his mid-thirties, he was sincerely religious and had gone on the pilgrimage a year or two before. Like most hajis, wore a beard. With a gentle face and an equally gentle sense of humour, he was a fund of practical, useful information. In the adjoining village, a new mosque was being built, and I asked who was paying for it.

'All of us, everybody in the village,' Ibrahim replied, giving the lie to the Istanbul intelligentsia who, disturbed by the resurgence of Islam in a declared secular state, claim that the new mosque-building in the villages is merely an act of self-aggrandisement of rich individuals. I found Ibrahim's reply to be much nearer the truth whenever I asked all over Turkey. There is talk of fundamentalism in Turkey, but wherever I became aware of an Islamic resurgence, which was not infrequent, it was neither radical nor revolutionary, merely a return to mosque-going and the security of faith that had been set aside in the heady days of Atatürk's Turkish political experiment.

In the evening, I would dine beside the lake in

restaurant gardens with a visiting American archaeologist and his wife, doing photographic site surveys from a twenty-foot-long balloon, a miniature Zeppelin, or with an English couple who stopped in the town for a couple of days. One evening I was picked up by a couple of counter clerks from the bank at which I changed my English currency and was taken off for a glass of beer. We discussed the difference between Turkish and English prices and salaries; the excellent beer cost 20p but the clerks' monthly salaries were only around £70. The countryside was idyllic and the people of infinite kindness, but the delay was frustrating and even a week of gentle exercising proved too much for the wretched new pony.

Late one night, Haji Ibrahim called at the hotel as I had not ridden, and I told him that as the horses were all too small for me, I must consider buying a horse and cart. At this moment Yusuf reappeared and the three of us went down to a lakeside *kahveci* for a council of war. It was eleven o'clock, but the whole town appeared still to be promenading as we discussed the problem. Ibrahim, who was hugely amused by the idea, kept bursting into fits of laughter.

'What an idea, James *amca*, what an idea!' Whether he thought it was a good idea or just very funny, I could never quite make out.

Even Yusuf, cured of his earache at last, thought it was funny, though it did not take him many days to use it as an excuse for further complaints as it did not fit into the image he had created for himself. He had latched on to the English expression of a 'gentleman jockey', and gentleman jockeys did not drive farm carts. Ibrahim told us that there was a horse fair at İnegöl, twenty-five miles away, the following morning, so we agreed to set off at eight.

The fair was in a field at the edge of the town. A largely gipsy throng stood around with their horses and carts of varying shapes and sizes, putting them through their paces for potential purchasers. Local farmers corralled bewildered groups of sheep or manoeuvred protesting cattle in and out of lorries. Argument and the inevitable glasses of tea flowed, broken by shouts and hearty handshakes to complete a deal, in which all the bystanders as well as the buyers and sellers seem to have partaken.

Within an hour, I had bought a local cart with pneumatic tyres and a half-Haflinger pony for £650, complete with harness, substantially less than I had paid for the disaster from Izmir. Brakes and a canopy for the cart were put in hand and the horse shipped back to İznik. Ibrahim, Yusuf, the vendor and I then retired to a celebratory lunch in İnegöl, plates piled high with İnegöl kofta, the local delicacy of roasted ground meat on a skewer.

When I refused a second large helping, Ibrahim chided me, with a grin, 'You are not much of an eater and you don't even drink much', which was quite untrue as I had consumed an enormous plate of meat and gallons of tea, but could cope with no more, good though it was.

By half-past six a blacksmith had been brought from Bursa to fit new *lastik naller*, horseshoes combined with slices of car tyre to provide both a grip on asphalt roads and shock absorbers between the hooves and the iron

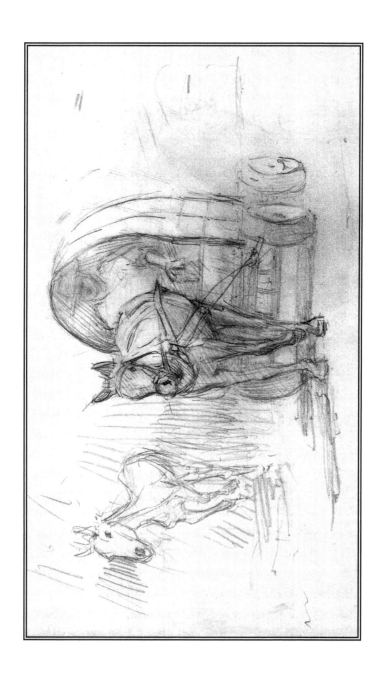

shoes. The bank in İznik even stayed open an extra hour to cash my traveller's cheque and the tellers fed me with nuts and ice cream while they did so.

Yusuf then sold the two old horses to a gipsy at a very poor price without consulting me, and the gipsy proceeded to welsh on the deal, walking off without paying £65 of the poor price agreed. Gipsies in Turkey also call themselves Romanies or Roman, and have the same reputation as elsewhere in the world.

The blacksmith in İnegöl had promised the work on the cart would be done in a week, and so we set off with the new horse and Ibrahim's taxi for İnegöl. Yusuf insisted on a spare horse and found one at a small town en route, which he drove in a cart for an hour or two and came on to join us at İnegöl, full of its praises, so I bought it and we lorried the two of them the last twelve miles to a gipsy-owned stable in the town.

Yusuf was becoming progressively more tiresome. His accounts had become more and more erratic and unlikely, so when he rushed into my hotel room at six o'clock in the morning demanding two months' pay immediately in order to go to Istanbul, I let fly. He had already been paid up to mid-July and it was now only mid-June, and I was getting very tired of it. He came back later in the day to say he had arranged for the blacksmith's mate to stand in for him as far as Eskisehir, while he had two or three days off. He then departed, but without any more money.

The next few days were busy and entertaining. There was the new horse to shoe with the rubber-and-iron shoes, and equipment to be bought for camping, like cooking utensils, a small stove, a lamp for inside the cart, spanners and screwdrivers for running repairs, all of which involved the delightful blacksmith, his mate and I in endless tours of the friendly little town.

I spent hours in the blacksmith's shop, watching his deftness of hand, and with the saddler who made minor repairs to the harness. The painter came to paint the traditional flower patterns and country scenes on the cart, all freehand, but with a certainty of stroke acquired by years of practice. There is great pleasure in watching good craftsmen at work, and in an era of mass production, it is a rarity, a thing forgotten. The Bursa blacksmith came to shoe the spare horse, full of friendly greetings and good wishes for the rest of the journey. In Turkey the two crafts of shoeing horses and other ironwork are separate trades with separate names: *nalbant*, a shoe smith; and *demirci*, an iron worker.

Finally – although not, of course, within the prescribed week – everything was ready and we planned an early start the following morning. The cart was shiny, pristine and glorious with beautifully painted red bodywork enlivened by roses, lake and mountain scenes, and swimming swans. The canopy was a brilliant blue canvas-textured plastic with clear plastic windows inset. To celebrate and to thank the blacksmith for all his assistance I took him and his mate to dinner in a good little restaurant that I had discovered the night before. The food was excellent, the party cheerful and spirited, and the drink very strong. By the time we had finished the second bottle of raki, we were reduced to a fit of hysterical giggles that lasted, uncontrollable, for a quarter of an hour. We staggered off home, still laughing and promising to be at the workshop at half-past six.

I cannot remember when we eventually assembled, but it was certainly not at half-past six. We lumbered about slowly, performing our allotted tasks with an extraordinary clumsiness. We decided to try out Yusuf's spare pony for the start. Nothing, neither whip nor kindness and patience, would get it to work. In fact, I never, ever got it to work. Yusuf had been completely conned and so had I, for I had paid for it. The gipsy vendor had given it a pre-med tranquilising injection before giving it to Yusuf to drive.

We changed over to Dobbin, the Haflinger cross, and got away at eleven. We moved very slowly, with Dobbin going all day and the spare pony tied to the back of the cart. It was hot and heavy and by early afternoon a thunderstorm burst, so we sheltered under a bridge and ate a lunch of fruit, bought that morning in İnegöl. The rain lightened and we set off again, grateful for the cool, but within an hour, the spare pony had broken its halter and galloped off, weaving in and out of the heavy lorries on the road. Horrified, I could do nothing but cover my eyes with my hands, but a few minutes later it returned unharmed, and thereafter walked placidly behind the cart. The road, however, was steep, rising steadily between pine-clad mountains, and at six, we pulled off onto a track leading down to a river to camp comfortably on its bank.

We were on the road by seven the following morning

and by eleven it was very hot again and the road even steeper. Dobbin was flagging, so we rested him for an hour or so in a lay-by and again tried the spare pony, with as little success as before. We stopped again at a roadside *kahveci* for lunch. By five, we thought we had all had enough and pulled off the road into a poplar plantation, and the amiable, if silent, blacksmith's mate hitched a lift back home as he had a wedding to go to the following day. I groomed and tethered the horses, got out the bread and sausage I had kept for my supper and walked off to the river, two hundred yards away, for water. Upon my return, a large, skinny sheepdog had appeared and my supper had vanished. It slunk around sheepishly and looked so hungry, I gave it some cheese as well and was fiercely guarded for the rest of the evening.

With the morning came steady, drenching rain. I fed and watered the horses and then breakfasted on a glass of tea (all that remained after the previous evening's canine visitation), and started up the steep, curving track back to the main road. As I led Dobbin by the head, he slipped on the greasy surface and slowly, inexorably, horse and cart slithered backwards off the track and the cart overturned. It might have been a piece of slow-motion, silent film. Muddy streamlets ran through the prostrate cart, covering everything with silt and slime. Strangely, Dobbin remained upright in the shafts, relatively unmoved by the experience, and the spare pony stayed attached to the rear of the cart, undamaged, if startled.

I stared for a minute or two at the devastation and started to unload the contents, stacking them in heaps in the pouring rain. Apart from the glass for the gas lamp, there was no damage, except to my self-esteem, and with the help of the shepherd owner of my dog friend of the previous night, I righted the cart, reloaded and packed the soggy contents and was off again. Within an hour, I was through Bozüyük and onto the Anatolian Plateau. But the cart had decidedly lost its virginity, its pristine beauty hidden under a layer of sticky mud. Dobbin plodded slowly but steadily on, mesmerised by the white line at the edge of the road, which he followed like a tramline. We stopped and camped at Inonu.

This area, where the old imperial roads debouch onto the plateau, is the site of one of the greatest battles of the First Crusade, the Battle of Dorylaeum. The exact site is disputed and a number of theories have been propounded, but it was certainly within a radius of five or ten miles of that evening's campsite. To alleviate the problems of supply, the crusading armies had divided into two and the leading force, under Bohemond of Taranto, was surrounded, on a hot July morning, by hordes of Turkish horsemen who, following their traditional pattern, swirled around the crusaders, maintaining a continuous fire of arrows and javelins without coming close enough to allow the heavier armour and horses of the knights to be used to advantage.

However, the sultan believed he had encircled the entire army, and when the second body arrived and a third smaller party descended from the hills in the rear, the Turks lost their nerve and fled, abandoning the sultan's tent and the remainder of his treasure that had survived the capture of İznik. He never again tried seriously to confront the crusade, and it was not until several years later, when the Turks caught and defeated another crusading army, smaller and less ably led, in the same location, that Seljuk's self-confidence was restored. But it had been a close thing, and crusader chronicles record an admiration of the fighting qualities of their Turkish opponents.

Nine hundred years later, my reception was different. The *muhtar* of Inonu, a somewhat romantic, gipsy-esque figure, with a horse of his own which he kept purely for pleasure, found me a stable and the villagers loaded me with gifts of bread and fresh milk and stopped by to ask endless questions. At this altitude, around three thousand feet, the crops were a couple of weeks behind those of İznik, the fields of wheat were still green and the cherries as yet unripe.

As I had now neither seen nor heard anything of Yusuf for five or six days, I caught a bus to Eskisehir to leave a message for him at the bus station, and returning, found the contents of the cart spread everywhere. Suspecting some new but incomprehensible disaster, I ran towards it to discover it was merely the errant Yusuf, who had arrived in my absence and was drying out and cleaning the contents. I had been once more on the point of sacking him.

It had become hot again, so we waited until the evening and then drove for a couple of hours on into the mountains on the road to Kütahya, a tiring trip in the residual heat of the day, where on the steeper stretches, one of us drove while the other put his shoulder to the back of the cart in an attempt to ease Dobbin's burden.

We were, therefore, grateful to find a mountain spring bubbling out into a drinking trough on the hillside where we could camp. It began to rain again, and from the comfort of our tents, we listened to the sounds of sheep bells and the drumming rain.

The rain continued all night and until midday the following day. We started early, but after three hours of difficult driving, halted at a petrol station for food. The road had been very steep and the rain unrelenting; to ease the load, I had walked most of the way and had pushed again on the steepest slopes, leaving Yusuf, being the lighter, to drive. We were drenched, but after an hour, I wanted to go on. Yusuf would not, so I left him while I found stabling in the adjoining village and drank tea and coffee with the village schoolmaster and his bright young daughter, who spoke a little English. I returned to the campsite, a sea of mud beside a noisy main road, to find Yusuf had got drunk on vodka sitting in the cart. He announced that he was quitting and rang the Jockey Club to say so and was promptly told that, if he did, there would be no job for him either at the racecourse at Istanbul or Izmir. I divided the rest of the day between a damp tent and the rather depressing petrol station restaurant.

Within an hour of starting on the following morning, both horses were lame, so we stopped at the first possible place, a small Shiite village whose inhabitants had come originally from Khorasan. Turkey is full of such villages. The slow disintegration of the Ottoman Empire and the Russian expansion into Central Asia in the nineteenth and early twentieth centuries produced a steady flow of Turkish-speaking Muslim refugees who were settled in Anatolia or Cilicia – Tatars from the Crimea, Circassians from the Caucasus, Uzbeks and Kipchaks from Central Asia and more recently, after the Greco-Turkish war of 1922–3, many more from the Greek islands and mainland. Atatürk himself came from Salonika. It continues to this day with the new exodus from Bulgaria, and the Turkish government, much to their honour, always accepts them. What upheaval drove these very poor villagers from their original homes, whether the Tsars or the Communists, I was unable to find out, but they brought their kindness and hospitality with them.

Yusuf caught the bus back to Yenişehir, where he had found the dreadful spare horse, to see a horse dealer, while I went the other way to Kütahya to go to the bank. The village was too poor to have its own *kahveci* and on my return, I found myself making tea for half the village in the back of the cart. My Turkish wireless, which was unable to get the BBC, was commandeered for the entire evening.

I took a used bus ticket to Kütahya from my pocket, which was seized and welcomed, and when I asked, 'To claim against KDV?' (the local VAT), they burst out laughing and said, light-heartedly, I must be a government spy!

For lack of a *kahveci*, they sat under the eaves of the building I was allotted as a stable, where a Bairam card from the adjoining village was pinned to the corner post supporting the overhang. Generous supplies of bread and excellent fresh yoghurt appeared, two or three times what I could eat, and there was great interest in my cooking of my usual vegetable stew. The party under the eaves, lit by my gas lamp, lasted until ten and at half past ten yet more yoghurt was thrust in a bowl through the flap of the cart canopy.

The morning was a joy: no rain and no Yusuf. I did my washing early in a small river beside the village and then followed it down the valley to a reservoir half a mile away. Bare hills rose sharply from the water's edge and the shallows were full of storks stalking frogs and minnows with their strange, ungainly movements. Sheep bells echoed back across the water and two horse teams with small carts were loading hay in the fields along the riverbank. All the carts in the village were pulled by pairs of ponies, for they doubled up pulling carts or ploughs.

In the evening, a pump for an airbed that I had bought in İnegöl came in useful to pump up the village football, and as the bed had already been irreparably punctured, I gave it to the village, pleased that, for once, I could return a kindness. In the early hours of the morning, Yusuf appeared in a lorry, loaded up the horses and disappeared again, leaving me to follow him back to Yenişehir at a more acceptable hour.

He had found a horse at Yenişehir, another strangely coloured Haflinger cross, creamy with black socks, which looked good. He, however, had had enough and asked for ten days off, having found a gipsy substitute. I was delighted. Rafet, the gipsy, could not be worse or more depressing than Yusuf. We arrived back at the village at eight, just in time to set up a tent before dark, but a spaghetti supper took longer and I forgot the remainder of the food outside. Again, the dogs had the lot. In my absent-mindedness, I was becoming quite a favourite with Turkish dogs.

The kind villagers refused any sort of payment for the stable and Rafet and I set off with Dobbin Mark II through a barren and tortuous range of mountains, without water or villages. Dobbin II went well and Rafet drove most of the morning with assurance and certainty. But it was hot again, if relieved by an occasional breeze, and at the end of four and a half hours, the pony had had enough. We reached another petrol station and halted in an adjoining field, wedged between the busy main road and a tree-lined river at the bottom of a narrow gorge. We had only covered twelve miles, but in that terrain, it was all we could manage, so we lazed away the rest of the day in the shade of the trees and in the petrol station restaurant. There I fell into conversation with a potter from Kütahya who made İznik tiles and had had an exhibition of his work in Paris. The following month he was to have another in England. He had stopped for a glass of tea and I told him of the kindness I had met at the Shiite village. He had bought a patch of land there and was just starting to build himself a house on it.

'Yes,' he said, 'they are good people and absolutely honest. And the place is beautiful, I love it. Oh, when you get to Kütahya, look me up and I will help you with stabling.'

The night was cold with a heavy dew and sleep was interrupted by large trucks passing every couple of minutes. We pressed on early, but the road was more difficult than ever for the first two hours and, as we pushed an exhausted Dobbin relentlessly along the last, more level stretch into Kütahya, we were both anxious lest he too should fall lame. He was proving to be an amiable and playful creature, who nibbled at my clothes for attention. We tied him to a lamp standard in the main street and set off to look for Sitki Olcar, the potter.

We found him in his workshop and joined him for lunch. He called in an English-speaking friend to interpret and the local reporter from *Hürriyet*, a leading daily paper. In the adjoining first-floor room, half a dozen girls were painting pots, while below us, on the ground floor, men were preparing clay and loading a kiln. Kütahya is the only place left in Turkey where such pots and tiles are still made, varying in quality from quite beautiful to the most excruciating tourist trash, but all following the traditional patterns. Sitki's tiles were lovely and I was to spend many hours in the course of the next week, watching the processing.

We brought the cart up to the back of the workshop and took Dobbin off to a cavernous caravanserai in the centre of the town, beneath a *kahveci* in a cobbled courtyard. The *Encyclopaedia of Islam* lists the virtues of Kütahya in the late nineteenth century, when one-third of the population was either Greek or Armenian. The list includes twenty-four mosques, twenty-one Islamic schools, sixteen Dervish monasteries, nine caravanserais or *hans*, eleven baths, twelve potteries, four churches and two libraries. From this I would assume that the inhabitants were holy, well scrubbed, well read and well heeled. Not a lot has changed since then, however, except for the departure of the Greeks and Armenians and the abolition of the Dervish monasteries. The older part of the town lies huddled around the foot of a small mountain, still crowned by the ruins of a Byzantine castle, and the old trades are still plied in the same places. Saddlers fixed my harness and shoemakers resoled my shoes with slices of car tyre, and in the hotel, I managed to have my first bath for a week.

But I still had problems. The cart was obviously too heavy for the type of terrain that I had to cross, and needed to be replaced with something lighter. Rafet said he knew where to get one and left for home to see his sick wife, promising to return in a couple of days. I wandered around the town, looking at the attractive traditional architecture; found a charming early fifteenth-century mosque, wrote letters, rested and talked to Sitki until Rafet's return. Sitki's family was an ancient one, of Seljuk origin, and had lived in Kütahya for centuries, but they now had little land and his passion was the recreation of İznik tile-making techniques, and his particular pride was the discovery and reproduction of the lost İznik red colouring.

Rafet's return was startling. He appeared early one morning and I discovered that my cart had disappeared and a small and somewhat dilapidated substitute stood there in its place, without seat, canopy or half the saddlery and the tools. I blew up and was gently reprimanded by Sitki's English-speaking friend, saying that the fault was largely mine, as I should be much more selective in my friends! But, after threats, the canopy and some of the missing saddlery were returned and with help from the delightful Sitki, the new cart was repaired, a seat installed, the canopy cut down to fit and a chain and shoe brake added. But I had had enough of whingeing Yusufs and thieving gipsies and decided to carry on hereafter by myself.

Sonnet Written in Istanbul

My mind is too disordered to explain
That meeting of two ships upon a sea
Of joint distress. It lit such flames in me
Of joys and sorrows, sympathy and pain
I thought that we would never steer again
Except to shipwreck: while I sought to be
Some succour in the storm where, safely, we
Could shelter for a day and thus regain
Self-mastery. But I could not restore
A quietude, a peace, as fresh waves tore
At moorings, new passions buffeted at sails.
I claim no credit now that calm prevails:
A wiser head than mine restored to reason
Typhoon emotions of that storm-filled season.

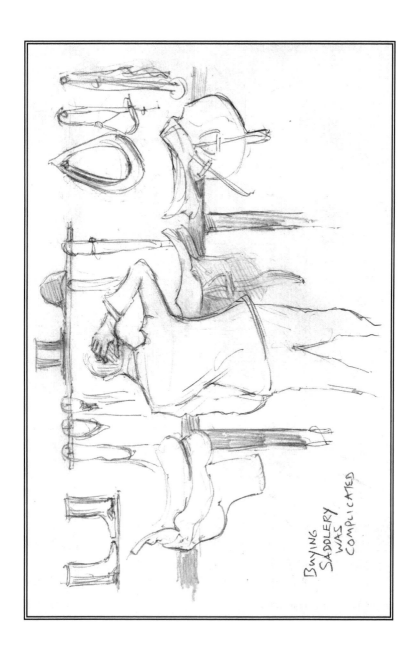

BUYING
SADDLERY
WAS
COMPLICATED

III

Anatolia

I left Kütahya late, having waited an hour or so for the reporter from *Hürriyet*, who wanted photographs, but never turned up. I had enjoyed my stay, for it is an attractive and friendly town but is not be recommended for its culinary excellence; good cooking was obviously not one of the subjects that had come down with the heritage of the twenty-one Islamic schools, or *medressehs*. Their curriculum was obviously more concerned with the mind and the soul than the body, a sadness for gourmets such as me.

The day was cool with a cold wind as the road led me across rolling hills, sparsely cultivated. By mid-afternoon, Dobbin had slowed noticeably, for some of the hills were quite steep, so I stopped by an ancient mosque and a roadside fountain, the first buildings I had passed since leaving the town, twenty miles back. A tiny orchard beside the mosque provided a good campsite and I tethered Dobbin on a long rope to allow him to graze, before sheltering in the lee of a derelict building to make tea.

A hay cart, drawn by a pair of ponies, approached the corner of the orchard. Dobbin rushed excitedly towards them, throwing the pair into confusion so, abandoning the tea, I ran forward to restrain him. The next thing of which I was aware was trying, drunkenly, to pick myself up off the ground, spitting out broken teeth and blood. Dobbin's well-shod hoof had caught me on the point of my chin, splitting it and breaking a couple of teeth. It was two or three minutes before I could stand upright.

The driver of the hay cart dismounted and pointed me in the direction of a petrol station, three hundred yards away, saying, as he drove off, 'They will give you first aid at the petrol station.'

I picked up my own St John Ambulance first-aid pack and staggered to the petrol station, where the two attendants, delighted at the diversion from the normal tedium, cheerfully helped to patch me up and dosed me with the inevitable tea. Shocked and in increasing pain, I returned to the orchard, fed and watered Dobbin and retired to bed in my tent. Eating was impossible, so I poured myself a strong glass of raki from the bottle I kept in the cart as a painkiller.

I awoke at five the following morning and had difficulty in raising my head off the ground, such was the pain. Outside the tent, I found that Dobbin had pulled up his eighteen-inch stake and had disappeared. However, I found him within half an hour, grazing a few hundred yards away, and we were off by half-past six.

I drove through scantily scrub-covered or barren hills, devoid of people or animals, for four hours, until I came to the next petrol station and restaurant. I managed to drink a little tea and a bowl of soup and, deciding that I had had enough for the day, drove a further mile off the road to the nearest village, where some young men kindly found me a stable and opened up the village guest room, before dispersing in search of tea and *ayran*. The guest-house keeper, a very wizened old man, soon appeared with the tea and produced a meal, but I was unable to eat anything but the yoghurt. Feeling very sore and groggy, I slept until the villagers came in to talk in the evening and then struggled to make conversation until they left for the evening prayers at half-past ten.

The next day began even earlier. I was out on the road before six o'clock, drifting across great sweeps of empty landscape, with acre upon acre of drying wheat and barley already burnt yellow and awaiting harvest. Hollyhocks, creeping hibiscus and blue cornflowers grew wild by the roadside, and in the distance herds of sheep moved in a haze of dust to a chorus of bells. The morning had begun quite cold, but by half past ten, it was hot. I stopped at another petrol station for tea and to check on Dobbin, as the night before, he had shown signs of a small harness gall under his horse collar, but it was no worse. Telling my tale to the restaurateur as I drank my tea, produced gasps of astonishment.

'From Istanbul, *mashallah*, and going to Jerusalem! *Cok, cok zor*, very, very difficult!' he exclaimed. I was beginning to agree with him.

I stopped after twenty miles, at a village set, like most of them, a mile or so off the road. A solid, genial, middle-aged man led me to the village guest room, which adjoined a stable. A Gastarbeiter in Hamburg for fourteen years, he had recently returned home to his village and a comfortable retirement. He had accumulated enough savings to live off his land and become a person of consequence.

'It was very interesting,' he told me, 'but I never liked the Germans; they are such egoists.' He left me to rest for an hour and then returned with a light lunch of yoghurt and soft vegetables that my battered jaw could cope with. We then toured the village; the mosque, the shops, a caravanserai that he claimed was Seljuk, but whose door looked earlier to me, Byzantine, perhaps.

The caravanserais, or *hans* in Turkish, were established by the Seljuks at twenty-five-mile intervals, a day's journey, along all the main trade routes. The greatest of them remain, part ruined, as monuments of Seljuk architectural taste; only the austere stone walls and single ornately carved doorways are visible from the outside. Inside, huge, vaulted stables surround a courtyard and a little mosque, while above are rooms where the travellers could store their goods and sleep in safety at the end of the day's travel. Under the Ottomans, *hans* proliferated, but without the aesthetics; more renowned for their fleas and dirt than elegance, they nevertheless provided the necessary safe accommodation and services for the traveller until the advent of motor transport. Now they have vanished, to be replaced by the ubiquitous petrol station and associated restaurant, except in the larger towns where one dilapidated *han* often still exists to accommodate farmers and their beasts on market days.

Then my mentor, Suleyman, led me to the chemist.

My broken teeth had been causing me considerable pain and the chemist, with a dentist's drill in a grubby workshop, filed off the sharp edges, refusing any form of payment. It was kindness, kindness everywhere, and as I had, by now, acquired a smattering of effective Turkish, it was easier as I was not so tongue-tied in my appreciation.

Towards dusk, we wandered out into the fields, where shepherds were driving in their sheep and old crones came home with flocks of geese that followed behind them like so many dogs. The immensity of sky resembled East Anglia, but with hills; the whole landscape had an austere grandeur and beauty that became, as we walked, accentuated by the sunset catching and gilding the thin streaks of cloud. My own delight in it pleased Suleyman, a man with an aesthetic sense; to share the pleasures of his surroundings with an appreciative stranger gave him an unexpected satisfaction, an added pride in his surroundings. We returned to the *kahveci*, outside which a farmer was showing off a new and brightly painted cart. Turkish farm carts and the designs painted on them are regional and distinctive; mine originated from Konya, where they build simple flat carts with four foot-high boards around them to retain the load, traditionally painted with brightly coloured geometric designs. Those from Bursa are deeper and half-barrel-shaped with bench seats in the front, and painted with flowers and country scenes not dissimilar to the traditional patterns on English canal boats. All are well sprung with elliptical springs and many now have pneumatic tyres.

The Turks had all taken to Mrs Thatcher, who had visited Turkey a couple of months before, and she was an endless source of curiosity. Suleyman had already declared his interest in politics.

'What do you think of Thatcher?' A woman Prime Minister to a Turk is almost inconceivable.

'*Bir kadin ama iki erkek gibi* (A woman, but like two men),' I replied.

'We could do with her here,' came the reply.

The muezzin's call to prayer woke me at half-past four. It seemed to echo through the whole expanse of Anatolia, a human cock-crow waking the faithful to pray from village to village across a thousand miles. The morning was still warm and heated up very quickly. I drove until eleven, when the temperature had reached the nineties, and then stopped at a restaurant to rest Dobbin and for something to eat, but I found that it was still too painful to eat anything more solid than yoghurt.

After half an hour's break, I pressed on towards Afyon, but soon Dobbin was reacting to neither word nor whip, so I stopped again to discover a large harness gall underneath his collar. I was five miles from Afyon, on the edge of its oasis of orchards, so I unharnessed him in a shady lane and, after an hour's rest, set out to find a stable. Two extremely ill-mannered youths said they would help and then demanded money. They started to lead me to the nearest village, then thought better of it and stopped to sit under the shade of some trees. The village, a mile further on, had no stable and an equally unhelpful *muhtar*, so I walked for a further two hours, in intense heat, leading a very tired Dobbin to a *han* in the centre of the town. I found a clean and comfortable hotel, which is more than could be said for the *han*, but the people at both were kindly and helpful.

The telephone rang at five o'clock in the morning. It was Yusuf, demanding immediate attention, accompanied by Rafet, the gipsy, and a slightly embarrassed Ibrahim, the taxi driver from İznik, who had driven them here. They had brought with them a bridle and numnah that Rafet had stolen, and after a further row, I paid off Yusuf with £200 and to ensure Ibrahim would not be out of pocket, paid the taxi fare of a further £50. They departed and I felt quite light-headed with the relief of getting rid of Yusuf and Rafet, if sorry for poor Ibrahim in his embarrassment. Exhausted by the heat and the continuing pain from my jaw, I slept for the rest of the morning before seeking out a vet to look at Dobbin's harness galls. He gave him an antibiotic and recommended two to three days' break to allow the wound to heal. A friendly carter offered to attach my cart to the back of his own and bring it into the town, so we cantered off and brought it to a cart-builder's yard for minor repairs.

With a few days' forced inactivity, I had time to get someone to look at my jaw, so I rang an old friend at Izmir, the senior British officer in the NATO base there, and invited myself to stay for a couple of days. The *han* keeper agreed to look after Dobbin and I took the bus to Izmir. Izmir was very hot and very humid, but I was met by my friends with a dinner designed for sore jaws, plenty of good whisky and a lot of English conversation.

I had not spoken more than a few sentences of English for a month. They had even arranged an appointment to have my jaw X-rayed, for I was afraid it might have been cracked, and joy of joys, we found an English bookshop, for I had been without reading matter for a couple of weeks. My jaw proved only to be badly bruised and after two further days of being gloriously cosseted, I returned to Afyon.

As Dobbin's collar had been the source of his problems, I spent the morning after my return finding a better-fitting replacement and we were away by two. It was much cooler, following a thunderstorm in the night, but the road was dreary. We plodded on through twenty kilometres of ribbon development factories, and when I pulled off the main road to a village, I found that Dobbin still had problems with galls. I discussed it with the villagers who had gathered in the guest room.

'Have you any felt?' asked one.

'I have a spare numnah.'

'That will do. If we cut a strip off that and sew it into the collar, thus,' he said, and set to work at once. Later, I was to discover the other Turkish remedy, which was to apply axle grease to the rubbed area. It works very well. The following day was better: I travelled twenty miles to Cay, the next town, and the felt lining in the collar worked well. Nevertheless, I decided to give Dobbin a day's rest.

Cay is a dull small town, but with a backdrop of the Sultandag Mountain and the well-treed greenery of its immediate surroundings, it was a pleasant contrast to the yellow-brown emptiness of the plain. It is enlivened by two poor restaurants, two billiard saloons and a rather dull, mid-thirteenth-century, Seljuk *medresseh*. The only *han* had closed down, but the blacksmith had a stable and sent his young son off for fodder on his moped, as I had run out. The young boy spoke, surprisingly, quite understandable English, and when I took him and a friend off to reward them with an ice cream, he protested mildly that, as I was the visitor, he should be buying it for me. English speakers are a rarity in Turkey and the best I found in the villages were almost always young teenagers from the Anatolian High Schools. These schools, of which there are now nearly a hundred, resemble, in some ways, English grammar schools but are language-based, starting by giving eleven-year-olds a year of intensive English and, judging from the products that I met, are highly successful.

Having a day to spare, I caught a bus to Konya, which I had given as a poste restante address. There was one letter and a book, sent by my English acquaintances from İznik. There had been others, but as I was over two months behind schedule, these had all been returned to sender. This was to be the only mail I was to receive in eight months of travelling.

I was half an hour down the road from Cay before I realised that I had left my radio with the blacksmith, but as I could not get the BBC on it and he was both very poor and very kind, it seemed appropriate, so I carried on. It was hot again and the road full of heavy traffic, so I stopped at midday and did not move on again until the evening, when the worst of both heat and traffic had passed. The road was lined with orchards, in front of which, farmers had erected stalls, heaped with apricots and bitter cherries. They waved and shouted greetings as I passed.

At dusk, I pulled in at a very grand-looking petrol station to find that it was closed for refurbishment. However, the caretaker welcomed me and, tethering Dobbin in the adjoining orchard, I erected my tent and joined him for tea. Some of his friends appeared and we sat in the orchard under a canopy of brilliant stars and talked till late, feasting on more tea and the fruit that I had brought on the road; a cheerful party.

From the petrol station to Akşehir was only twelve miles and I reached it by mid-morning. The road had again been full of traffic and the worn tarmac surface as smooth as glass. On the slopes, Dobbin had slipped and slid all over the road and had become correspondingly nervous. As Büyük Bairam, the greatest Islamic feast of the year celebrating the sacrifice of Abraham, was only a week away, most of the traffic had been German-registered cars, filled with expatriate Turks returning for the holiday. In the course of the coming week, I was to count them and found that almost two out of three of the passing cars were foreign-registered; the Turkish expatriate community were obviously prosperous and every village seemed to have men working somewhere in Europe.

I parked both horse and cart in the *han*, threw my saddlebags over my shoulder and climbed up the hill behind the town to a tourist hotel, where I could have a bath and get my laundry done. Both were very necessary. Having made myself slightly less offensive to the public's nostrils, I walked down the hill again to Nasreddin Hodja's tomb and its surrounding garden.

Nasreddin Hodja is both a myth and a reality; that this archetypal wise fool and joker lived here in the thirteenth century is almost certain, but if he had not, it would have been necessary to invent him, for he is the consummation of peasant wit and wisdom. How many of the endlessly popular Turkish jokes and stories really relate to the man buried beneath the little *turbe* is immaterial. Whether he lived for a while at the court of Tamerlane as the legend would have us believe, or a hundred years earlier as the evidence would suggest, does not matter. What matters is that all the stories of that genre in Turkey have become Nasreddin stories; they are there, they are enjoyed and they are repeated ad infinitum. The Arabs have Goha, an identical figure but unattached to time or place, as far as I am aware.

One of the favourite Nasreddin tales is when his neighbour came to ask to borrow his donkey. Nasreddin, however, was unwilling to lend it, yet did not wish to offer a blunt and discourteous no.

'It isn't here, it is in the fields.'

At that moment, the donkey brayed in the stable behind the house.

'But I can hear it.'

'Well,' replied Nasreddin, in a feigned temper, 'if you prefer to believe the word of a donkey to that of its owner…!' There is an amusing statue of him, wearing an enormous turban and sitting on his donkey, in the middle of the roundabout facing the garden.

Back in the hotel, they were preparing for a party. Microphones and loudspeakers were being manoeuvred around the dining room and the broad terrace overlooking the town; there was an air of disorganised but enthusiastic industry. In the middle of this turmoil of cables and upset chairs, I found a don from Cornell University. He was an archaeological dendrologist and a fluent Turkish speaker, who was touring Turkey with three of his favoured students, dating buildings from the timbers in them.

His science was totally beyond my comprehension, but he was extremely well informed on all things Turkish and entertaining about them. We joined forces for the evening and sat on the terrace for dinner, to avoid the more claustrophobic din of the band inside. The meal finished with plates piled high with spectacularly flaming fruit. What the floods of burning spirit were intended to do to the already excellent fruit, I never quite understood, but it was certainly spectacular. Rather too much so for one young and excessively eager waiter, who managed to set light to both the fruit and himself. The hotel filled with a busload of German tourists and locals having their Friday evening out; the noise was tremendous, but the people who seemed to enjoy it most of all were the hotel staff. I retired to bed with the sound still pulsating down on the balcony below me.

I came down for breakfast at eight the following morning. The dining room remained untouched after the night's musical hurricane, and of the staff there was no sign. After an hour, the human-candle waiter appeared and sank woefully down behind the reception desk, unable to do much more than bewail his scorched face. Another waiter appeared half an hour later and, being without injury except for a hangover, managed to produce some tea.

I returned to the town and, with the help of a saddler whose shop was in the *han*, went in search of a blacksmith. With the slipping and sliding of the day before, I had decided that it was time to get Dobbin reshod with the rubber-lined shoes, the *lastik naller*. The blacksmith had never made or fitted them before, but as the saddler and I felt we knew enough to give him instructions, we set to. It was exceedingly hot and, during the fitting of the two front shoes, Dobbin was as docile as a lamb. But that, he thought, was enough. The three of us struggled for half an hour and got nowhere, so we stopped and called for cooling glasses of *ayran* from the teahouse in the corner of the yard. We started again, and a kick sent the blacksmith rolling over backwards into the opposite corner. We called in the lad from the *kahveci*, hobbled Dobbin's front feet and roped the back ones, but to no avail. Eventually we got the job done, with six people holding on to ropes or the pony, all sweating profusely and gasping in the struggle. The *kahveci* did more business in the subsequent half an hour than it normally would do in a week.

Then when I came to pay the *han* owner's charge for the night, the bill was twice as much as the hotel. If he had been on one of the ropes, I would have understood, but he was not. He was a portly gentleman of sixty-odd who left all the work to his shrivelled old assistant as he strutted around in a very European suit complete with gold albert. The pompous old rogue rooked me.

At six, Dobbin and I set off. It was cooler, but not much, and we camped by the usual petrol station as night fell a couple of hours later. By now the heat was becoming a problem. I could not get away before six in the mornings as before half-past five, there was not enough light to pack up and harness Dobbin, and by eleven, it would be almost too hot to travel further. With each morning, I still awoke to fears of further disasters that the first few months had led me to believe were to be a daily occurrence.

In an attempt to lighten Dobbin's load, I made another attempt to discard every piece of unnecessary kit, which resulted in a much tidier cart but no noticeable reduction in weight. I drove on past vast acreages of wheat and barley that were now being harvested by every age of instrument, from modern combine harvesters to scythes. The squares in the towns and villages began to fill up with grain, and it was heaped high on every building plot.

After two days, I reached Kadınhanı, a small market town, in mid-morning. The Büyük Bairam holiday was almost upon me and I was very short of money, so I visited all five banks in the town. In spite of *Change* notices in the windows, none of them would change a traveller's cheque, only foreign banknotes, in which they were doing a roaring trade with the expatriate Turks back for the holiday. I must, they said, go to Konya. I could find no satisfactory shady spot to leave Dobbin, so left him tethered in full sun in a builder's yard. I returned in the late afternoon to find him on point of collapse, which he did before I could find an alternative place in the shade. I struggled to release and revive him, while a crowd stood around uselessly, laughing or giggling, until the town blacksmith came and helped me to raise the poor beast to his feet and lead him away to his own stable. The builder, whose gang had not even thought of giving the poor horse any water, slightly shamefacedly invited me for supper, before one hotel opened in the evening and provided a clean room and a shower.

Dobbin was still not very fit in the morning, so I only drove him two or three kilometres and parked in the shade of a small plantation beside a restaurant. The plantation was filthy with refuse from the restaurant, but it was the only bit of shelter. The restaurant itself was as dirty as the copse behind it and the restaurateur unhelpful. A thunderstorm had been building up and as it broke, he sent a waiter out to tell me to move Dobbin out of the copse. I had been talking to him an hour or so earlier, when he had made no objection, so I refused until the storm was over, but the rain began again in the night and lasted several hours, so I wrapped the poor beast, rather inefficiently, in a poncho to keep him as warm and dry as possible.

Packing up a sodden tent at half-past five in the morning is not the most joyous start to a day, but the temperature rose fast in spite of the night's rain and horse, man and cart were all soon steaming like kettles. After an hour, the road turned down into a steep gorge and Dobbin, for no explicable reason, suddenly pulled straight out into the middle of the road, into the path of an oncoming bus. It missed us by inches and disappeared hurling volleys of abuse.

Two hundred yards farther on, I tried another suicide act; I lost concentration and ran the front wheel of the cart off the road and over the edge of the adjoining precipice but, fortunately, a projecting iron stake saved us from disaster. An hour later, I pulled into a road maintenance compound, where a few trees provided a little shade and in which Dobbin and I shared a watermelon for breakfast, slice by slice. Watermelons had become a favourite with both of us. My map showed a small village some way along the route, so I asked the compound caretaker how far it was.

'Oh, only about five kilometres,' he said, and I set off again. But the village did not materialise. There were two or three huts just off the road in an arid, shadeless nothing, but certainly no village. I cursed the caretaker soundly to myself, but it was obvious that he was not sure that he, as a custodian of the Turkish Republic's property, ought to let vagabonds in carts, particularly foreign ones, shelter under its trees. They might steal half a ton of asphalt or some other national asset with which he was charged, so it was easier to suggest that paradise was just around the corner and so remove this threatening figure onto somebody else's patch.

Paradise proved to be a long way off. I plodded on through a desolation of emptiness for a further twenty-two miles until, cresting a long, low ridge, I found a petrol station which looked down across the sunburnt plain to Konya, ten miles away. It was this view, nearly nine hundred years before, that had gladdened the hearts of the first crusaders. The ragged army had lost half its horses and many knights travelled on foot or rode oxen, while sheep, goats and dogs had all been pressed into service to carry the baggage. From this small height, they could see the green of the gardens that surrounded the city, and with that sight came the renewal of hope.

At that distance, in the strong afternoon light, what now remained of those gardens looked black rather than green, and were just discernible through the haze of dust. But the petrol station staff were the reverse of the night before: helpful, welcoming and charming. A hideous, half-built, concrete extension gave a modicum of shade for poor Dobbin until the evening, while the adjoining waste provided me with a site for my tent. Sitting on the veranda of the small restaurant, I was plied with tea, Coca-Cola and the usual questions.

'Where are you from? Are you married? How much did you pay for the horse? How much for the cart? How do you like Turkey?' Fortunately, nobody ever asked why I was doing it, because I would have difficulty in answering in any language and in Turkish, I would have found it impossible.

Maybe discretion or manners forbade the question of why, but I think it was mainly because such an eccentric *yabanci*, or foreigner, was obviously mad and those afflicted by God cannot be expected to explain their reasoning.

The three-hour drive into Konya was plagued by heavy traffic. Juggernauts rushed by, their wind shaking the cart and the fumes suffocating; the last of the expatriates returning for Bairam sped past to buy the last necessaries for the following day's feast; and I was driving, for the first time, in a major city. The outskirts were filled with drab concrete blocks of flats, but the roads were broad and easy; the narrow, twisting lanes of the old town centre, however, were a nightmare. It was with great relief that I finally forced my way through a crowded market into the relative calm of the only *han*. It was spacious with lofty, well-kept stables, an ample, cobbled courtyard, a cheerful *kahveci* and a barber who shaved me before I set out to find a hotel.

Tourism has found Konya, and vice versa. There was a room in a package tour hotel, surrounded by the worst sort of tourist shops and where a small glass of raki (state monopoly price TL4,200 per bottle) was TL3,000 per glass. Package tours are wheeled into Konya, whirled around the town, fed, watered and bedded, and poured back into their buses early the following morning. An English package tour had just arrived, and I was delighted at the prospect of speaking my own language again. But the tour rather resembled the one I had been on when I decided to do it on a horse.

'Oh,' said a whey-faced lady, when told I had come on a horse, 'we only have two weeks and with so much to see, we couldn't afford the time.' With my ego thus pricked, I decided that the company in the *han* was more interesting.

The next evening was better, for I found, on the succeeding day's tour, a couple who were lecturers at a minor American university in New York state, and kindred spirits. Together we ate and drank and talked, rather too much of each, but we enjoyed it, in spite of an irritating waiter who, when he brought us our drinks, insisted in talking in bad French or German, even when asked to speak in Turkish.

Ichabod, the glory of Konya, has departed, but it had its day, political, artistic and intellectual, as the capital of the Seljuk Sultans of Rum, in the thirteenth century. For fifty years it was ruled by enlightened sultans, great builders of mosques, *hans* and hospitals, who melded the arts of Iran into the coarser new styles of the nomadic tribes and, as a seat of learning, it gave birth to the Mevlevis, the whirling dervishes, whose mystical sect survived and influenced Turkish Islam until their abolition in 1925. Succumbing to the Mongol Empire in the middle of the century, it became a Mongol client state and both sultanate and town withered in dynastic anarchy. It is surprising, viewed from a modern and nationalistic stance, to discover that the court language of the Seljuks and all the philosophy and theology of the Mevlevi dervishes was in Persian, but there had been no Turkish written language. Turkish was first adopted as an official court language in the mid-thirteenth century, and then it incorporated a huge vocabulary of both Arabic and Persian words, the religious terminology of Islam and the cultural disciplines of Iran.

I took to the road again, the road to Karaman, where there was, the *han* keeper assured me, another *han*. It was a diversion from the proper route, for the First Crusade went east, not south. Dividing again into two, some turned down through the Cilician Gates to Tarsus and east again from there, while the main body travelled north-east to Kayseri, before turning south through the Anti-Taurus towards Antioch.

I already knew the Cilician Gates, the main road from Istanbul to south Turkey and Syria; it is precipitous, steep, narrow and solid with traffic. If the steepness did not kill Dobbin, a lorry coming fast around a blind corner certainly would. The road via Kayseri and Maras was, by repute, even steeper, so I decided to opt for the Karaman to Silifke route, which was almost legitimate, as the Emperor Frederick Barbarossa had travelled it and died on it on the Third Crusade.

Dobbin and I trundled slowly along the road to the next village. With the holiday celebrations in full swing, the ritual of family-visiting and feasting left little time for attending to extraneous visitors, so I moved on and camped by a friendly, if mosquito-infested, petrol station. There was no restaurant, so I fried eggs beside the cart and sliced another watermelon, before joining the attendants for tea and talk, as passers-by and villagers called in to exchange seasonal greetings and offer traditional sweets.

The morning brought an invitation to breakfast with the attendants and conversation resumed, delaying my start until eight. Immediately on the road, Dobbin shied at some imagined terror, got entangled with badly adjusted harness and fell, slewing the cart across the full width of the road. It took me some minutes to release him, set him upright and re-harness him, but the traffic was very light and patient with my dilemma and Dobbin appeared undamaged by the fall. By the evening, though, he was showing slight signs of lameness. I stopped for tea and removed Dobbin's bridle to let him eat, and on returning five minutes later, discovered he had moved the cart and in doing so had caught his foot in the bridle and smashed it.

I could not repair it and so replaced it with a spare English bridle, but without blinkers, and thus set off with some trepidation in the morning, lest Dobbin should shy at traffic approaching from behind us. I need not have worried: he behaved perfectly.

A further long, slow and empty day brought me to Karabekir, along a dead straight road without villages, shade, anything. I drove into the centre of the town and tethered horse and cart to a tree outside a *kahveci*. A genial and rotund farmer with a military moustache bounced out to greet me, shouting out to the world in general.

'We have a visitor, we have a guest – bring tea, come along, bring *ayran*.' I was seated at one of the tables facing the street and was liberally plied with both tea and *ayran*. A watermelon seller had a stall a few yards away, and large plates of sliced watermelon were placed and replaced before me.

'Go on, eat,' said my jolly friend. I did, with gusto, for at the end of a long, hot day, it is an ideal restorative.

The party was joined by a young Turk who spoke good English. He was a schoolteacher in Holland, back on holiday, who promised to bring his English-speaking Dutch girlfriend later, but in the event, I camped at the far edge of the village and he could not find me.

I deliberately refused an invitation to stay with one of the villagers as, given all the Bairam visitors, I was afraid of imposing, so one of the party suggested that I pitched my tent on some wasteland behind his house and led me there, rather wobbily, on a bicycle. I camped in a very thorny field and as dusk turned Haci Baba Dag, the adjoining mountain, a soft pink, he came out to the tent with supper of bread, meat and yoghurt. The cart already looked like a fruit stall, for before I left the *kahveci*, everyone had loaded it with watermelons and grapes.

I made an early start on the last twelve or so miles to Karaman and stopped after three hours at yet another petrol station for tea. However, with the Bairam festivities still in progress, the attached *kahveci* was closed. An oafish local decided to hitch a lift and, jumping up, quite without invitation, then began complaining that Dobbin was slow and tired and jumped down again. Dobbin was both tired and slightly lame. By midday, I had reached the centre of the town, to discover that the *han* had been pulled down two or three years before. A tout appeared and said he would find me a stable and show me the way to a hotel, so I unharnessed poor Dobbin and tied him to the only tree in the square, before following the tout to the nearest *kahveci*.

Negotiations were started and a carter agreed to stable and feed Dobbin for 75p per day, so I carried my saddlebags to one of the town's two hotels, harnessed the pony again and followed the carter's moped to his house, a mile away at the edge of the town. For this service, the tout had charged me £3 which, in a village, would have been provided, and more, as part of the natural courtesies and hospitality. My introduction to Karaman was not encouraging. The stable was cramped and airless but the owner and his family were warm and kindly; I was anxious about Dobbin's feet and they tried hard to reassure me.

The hotel staff too were welcoming, which was more than could be said for the bed: it had springs that leaped out and stabbed one viciously from unexpected angles, and the plumbing was even more erratic than usual.

> In Turkey, plumbing is an art
> At which the Turks are not too smart.
> When water flows across the floor
> And trickles underneath the door,
> We know the water soon will dry,
> So we don't care, the Turks and I.

It also suffered from plagues of mosquitoes: if I left the windows closed I fried; if open I became a favourite mosquito restaurant. I tried compromises and merely found that the mosquitoes seemed to like me even better fried.

Leaving Dobbin to rest, I caught a bus to Mut, halfway down the road to Silifke, to see what it was like, but this route was worse than the Cilician Gates and a thousand feet higher. The barren, waterless mountains and the views from the road as it winds its way through them are magnificent, as seen from a bus, but the prospect of driving a pony and cart through them was another matter. My heart sank. Mut, at only nine hundred feet above sea level, was a furnace. Being the last day of the Bairam holiday, the public gardens were full of people sitting drinking tea and soft drinks beneath the shade of gigantic plane trees; children splashed in the channelled stream and fountains, while the menfolk played dominoes or backgammon and the women just sat in groups and talked. I walked up the hill to the ruins of an Armenian castle that dominates the town, but oppressed by the heat, retired to a good little restaurant, where I was joined by a fellow traveller from the bus. He had just visited his in-laws and inspected his gardens there and, together, we ate an excellent lunch before catching the next bus back to Karaman.

At half-past nine that evening, the telephone rang in my bedroom.

'A friend of yours is down here and wants to speak to you urgently,' said the receptionist.

I was mystified – a friend, here in Karaman? I did not know anybody except the stable owner. I went downstairs to find the awful Yusuf waiting in the foyer. Having lost his name with the Jockey Club, they refused to allow him to work as a groom there and he wanted his job back with me. As I had already paid him for two months more than he had actually worked, he offered to work for expenses only. He was trying to redeem his reputation. Weakly, I said I would give him a chance.

I got the local vet to look at Dobbin, who prescribed lotions and potions for his lameness and recommended two weeks' rest. As most of the prescription was not available in Karaman, I was quite glad, momentarily, of

Yusuf's return and despatched him with some money to Istanbul. The day was oppressive and overcast and drawing money from my account with the Is Bank took over an hour and a half. By the time I emerged from the bank, the heaviness had turned into a thunderstorm and I was drenched in the hundred-yard dash back to the hotel. The aftermath of the storm was cooler but that night the mosquitoes intensified and I did battle with squadron after dive-bombing squadron. In spite of a gallant defence with towels, sheets, notebooks and anything else that came to hand, the mosquitoes won, through sheer persistence.

Karaman is a dull town in which you can see all there is to be seen in an hour. A much-restored castle encloses a small Roman theatre, now occasionally used for concerts, and there is a fine gateway to a Seljuk-period *medresseh*, late fourteenth century, where the first sign of Ottoman motifs, the Ottoman tulip, has woven its way into the decoration around the door, but its mosques are unimpressive. For two hundred years, it was the seat of the independent *beylik* of the Karamanoglu, a dynasty of extraordinary belligerence, who fought Seljuks, Armenians, Mamelukes, Mongols and Ottomans in turn. At its height, the state stretched from Antalya on the coast to Afyon, and although frequently suffering devastating defeats, it kept bouncing back for more punishment. It was also the first Turkish state to maintain its records in its native language.

For the next three days, I exercised Dobbin morning and evening and doctored his feet. I filled in the rest of the days by rereading books that I had finished a week or so before, playing four different kinds of patience and talking to the friendly hotel staff, but my limited Turkish vocabulary restricted the conversation. Loneliness and a sense of isolation are one of the penalties of travelling alone. I have almost always chosen to travel that way on the grounds that it is easier to get one person out of trouble than two, and that, if alone, one is forced to try to speak the language of the country and thus become more involved in the life around one. But the obverse comes when, through weariness of body or spirit, one no longer has the energy to become involved; the shutters fall and one sinks into a deeper isolation than ever.

I found the one good restaurant in the town, but eating there twice a day, even its excellent menu began to pall. The only variation to the monotony was when Dobbin, being exercised around a large, empty building plot, reared and brought both his forefeet down on my forehead; fortunately the new rubber-lined shoes softened the blow and I had nothing worse than a few grazes and half an hour's headache.

Yusuf returned on the afternoon of the fourth day and, having visited the stable, announced that Dobbin was suffering from worms. He also stated that there were no worm doses available in Turkey, except imported ones obtainable from Istanbul at about £100 per dose. I had noticed in the last week or ten days on the road that Dobbin had had an enormous appetite but lacked energy, but had not considered worms. We trooped back to the vet, who was obviously unaccustomed to demands for horse worm tablets, but looked up his pharmacopoeia and produced another prescription, which Yusuf refused to use. I told him to get on and try it and I would see what I could find in Izmir, as I had decided he could do the doctoring for a few days, while I returned to my friends, John and Janie, in Izmir for another three-day break.

I took the bus to Izmir, going up, in the first five hours, the road to Afyon, which had taken me three weeks to cover in the cart. Travelling away from, rather than into, the sun, a beautiful light produced by a rare pattern of clouds gilded the dust and the distance. The grandeur of Anatolia was reaffirmed, awesome and very humbling. I arrived at Izmir at midnight and stayed at a hotel, for John and Janie had moved to their beach house at Foça, fifty miles away up the coast. As soon as it was open, I again raided the English bookshop and followed them down to Foça later in the morning, with an armful of new books.

Upon my return to Karaman, I was greeted by Yusuf with the news that Dobbin was fit and ready to go, but on arrival at the stables in the morning, found that his feet had swollen up again. It was clear that Dobbin would have to be replaced. I despatched Yusuf back to the horse trader who had produced Dobbin to seek a replacement, and prepared myself for a further week or two's wait in Karaman, at least armed this time with a new batch of books.

With so much time to kill, I took another bus to Erdemli, along the coast east of Silifke, to get a better look at the road, for I already had doubts about it. The stretch from Mut to Silifke proved to be as difficult and spectacular as Karaman to Mut, and the coast road thereafter a travesty of the lovely stretch that I remembered from seven or eight years earlier. What had been a wild and beautiful coast of ruins had now disappeared under a refuse heap of tawdry tourist developments and camping sites. The bus inched its way along through traffic like a London rush hour and my favourite castle, Kiz Kulesi (the Maiden's Castle), set on a tiny island just off the shore, looked more like Blackpool. My mind was made up. I would send the cart on to Adana and, with the new horse, would walk from Karaman through the Taurus Mountains, thereby avoiding the problems of driving down that forbidding road, and the humidity and squalor of the coast. There is an ancient site just in from the coast known as Cennet Cehennem, Heaven and Hell, but only Hell seemed to remain. The temperature at Erdemli had touched the 100°F mark.

At Silifke, there is a large and dramatic castle, crowning a hill just behind the town. I knew it well and had photographed it some years before, as it was briefly, at the beginning of the thirteenth century, a Hospitaller castle which the Order of St John held as a fief from the Kings of Armenia. Alas for chivalry. The young, widowed Queen Isabella of Armenia, whose handsome but arrogant crusader husband, a younger son of the Prince of Antioch, had so despised and insulted his subjects that he had been murdered by her relatives, fled to the castle and to the protection of the Knights of St John, to escape from a proposed marriage to an Armenian cousin. The Knights welcomed her but, sadly, had few illusions about duties to damsels in distress; realpolitik was not

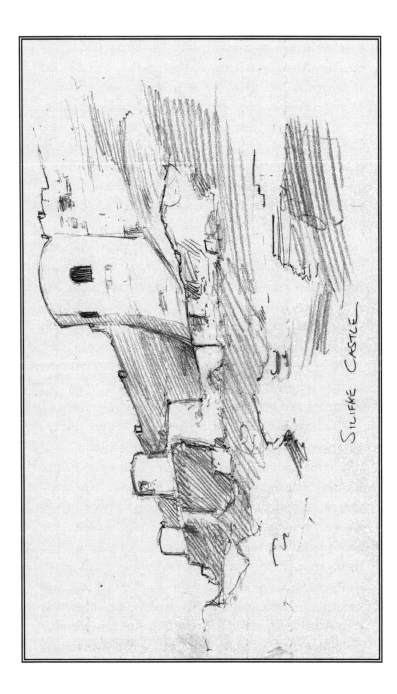

SILIFKE CASTLE

a nineteenth century invention except in name. The knights, having given her shelter, could not hand the poor girl over to her unwanted suitor, but were unwilling to involve themselves in an Armenian dynastic squabble. Thus, to mollify their somewhat doubtful consciences, they sold the castle back to the Armenian regent, the suitor's father, with the poor queen still inside. As the story goes, the couple lived unhappily ever after.

Yusuf rang from Istanbul while I was out exercising Dobbin, and left a message asking for £600 for the new horse and saying he was travelling to Erzerum to collect it. Having arranged the bank transfer, I wandered aimlessly around the town, desperately trying to kill time. The temperature stayed just short of 100°, with a hot, dust-laden wind shrivelling the last vestiges of green. On the outskirts of the town, long queues of lorries lined up daily by the railway station, waiting patiently in the stifling heat to transfer their golden heaps of grain into the infrequent goods trains.

I would start early in the morning, in the relative cool, doctoring and exercising Dobbin, and then continue walking, by myself, in an attempt to get fitter for the trip through mountains. With so little to occupy me, I had soon finished my new supply of books. Only the heat and lethargy softened the edges of frustration and boredom. I would sit for hours with Ayhan, the stable owner, his wife and children, but his Turkish was even more difficult than most. Although he was illiterate, his wife could read and write and his eldest son, having completed his secondary education, had now gone to a technical college. In spite of our inability to communicate except at the most basic level, we became friends; the whole family were so gentle, generous and friendly. I spent a morning unloading a cart full of tiles for repairs to his roof and gave him my spare saddle to make a little more space in the cart. Whenever I paid him for Dobbin's keep, he would protest mildly that it was too much and his wife would smile and come out of the house with another tray of tea or *ayran*, and they would often press me to stay for a meal.

Back in the hotel, I asked about the road across the mountains and was told to follow the Mara *yolu*, the Mara road. But my map showed no such town or village. In fact, my map showed almost nothing in between Karaman and Tarsus and it was only weeks later, when I got there, that I discovered that Mara was the old Armenian name for what had recently been Turkicised into Kırobası. I was assured that I would find everything in the *yaylas*, the nomad summer encampments in the mountains; neither fodder, food or even cigarettes would be a problem, but I was doubtful – I had heard these sorts of assurances before.

Bookless again, I thought I would try Ankara for a new supply and caught a midnight bus for the six-hour journey. It was a cramped, uncomfortable and a sleepless night but, by ten, I had found a bookshop, replenished my supply and caught a spacious, air-conditioned bus for the return trip. But on my arrival, I found poor Dobbin's face was a mess. The vet came, diagnosed dermatitis and gave me another prescription.

Yusuf arrived in the afternoon. He had been away a week, had seen the horse in Erzerum and had arranged

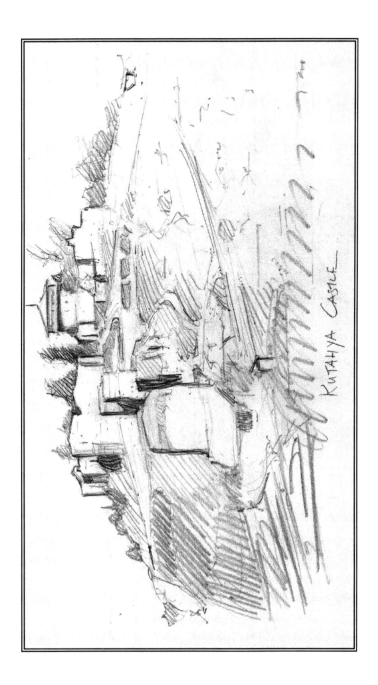

KUTAHYA CASTLE

for it to share a lorry to Adana. It was a half-Arab stallion called Murat, had cost £700 and was due to arrive at Adana in three days' time. Obviously bored by the prospect of sitting in Karaman, Yusuf made some excuse and vanished again, off to Adana, leaving me to continue doctoring Dobbin.

I retired to my room and started to read Virginia Woolf's *Orlando*, which I found rather a forced joke, but was grateful for any diversion. When that palled, I went downstairs and spoke to the nice, lame, young hotelier and talked about his business. It was run as a lodging house, with a television room-cum-salon where tea and coffee were brought in from the adjoining *kahveci* and there was a refrigerator behind the reception desk from which cold drinks were dispensed.

'You see,' he said, 'we are often full on Tuesdays, Wednesdays and Thursdays, but for the rest of the week, almost nobody comes, so we cannot afford to make any improvements. I would like to, but it is a question of money.'

As Ayhan and his eldest son had volunteered to apply Dobbin's dermatitis lotion and exercise him for a day or so, I decided to make a brief excursion to Cyprus. Ferries run from Taşucu to Kyrenia, now rechristened Girne, where I had holidayed years earlier, and Taşucu was only two hours away by bus. The hydrofoil ferry was very modern and immaculate; the captain invited me up to the bridge for the three-hour journey and explained its polyglot provenance. The hull was Australian, the engines German, the radar Italian, the echo sounder

Danish and the automatic pilot Canadian, a nautical United Nations. Visibility was poor and so we saw nothing until Girne and the surrounding mountains were suddenly upon us. The town had changed little in twenty years, except for the ritual statue of Atatürk now erected near the waterfront, and its charm was undiminished, but the heat and humidity even exceeded that of the mainland coast. I found a room in a small hotel and sank into a sweating stupor until the evening.

The relative cool of the evening revived me and I had promised myself an indulgence. On my last visit, I had found a very good, if somewhat expensive, restaurant on the waterfront in the old harbour. The Harbour Club Restaurant had been run by an Englishman and the cuisine was memorable. The patron and I had discussed our favourite Elizabeth David recipes and he introduced me to others that I have cooked, on and off, ever since. I returned to the waterfront and found the restaurant unchanged except for the owner. The Englishman's successor was a Turk who had run a restaurant in Chelsea for some years and then decided to return to the less pressured life of his hometown. The cooking was completely unchanged: it was excellent. As it was early in the evening, most of the tables were still empty, so he came to join me and talk.

'North Cyprus is really a satrapy of mainland Turkey,' he explained, in answer to my queries. 'Although the government proclaims its total independence, it is an illusion, a facade. We are totally dependent on Turkey economically and politically, so how can we be truly independent?'

We talked about the Islamic resurgence in mainland, Turkey and Turkish politics in general. He was highly critical of the mosque building.

'It is hypocrisy – how can they spend so much money on building new mosques, when there are not enough desks and chairs in the schools?'

'But what I have found is that the mosques are not government-funded, but are built by villagers and townspeople themselves. They want to restore their cultural roots. Surely, one of the failings of Atatürkism is that, while proclaiming the virtues, the pride and the uniqueness of being a Turk, it has cut off the race from its history by a combination of a new alphabet and the secularisation of the state? Though both of these things were logical and necessary, they have left an emotional hole that needs to be filled.'

'Perhaps, but what Turkey needs more than anything else is education. How can it compete in a modern world, without education?'

'I have been very impressed by the children from the Anatolian High Schools; their ability to speak English, for example, is remarkable.'

'But they are only open to the few, to the children of those with influence.'

'Yet I have found these children in villages – they were village children, not the children of rich Istanbulus.'

'I hope you are right,' he said.

Other diners began to appear and he left to greet them and take their orders, before returning to carry on the conversation, which wandered broadly from subject to subject. When I left, I was filled with the sense of well-being that comes from good food, good drink and good conversation.

The morning was hotter and stickier than ever, so I took a taxi up the mountain to Bellapaix to look again at that beautiful Gothic abbey and to escape the worst of the humidity until I had to return to catch the return ferry in the early afternoon.

I was back in Karaman by midnight, and at 2.30 that morning, Yusuf knocked on the door, asking for money for the lorry hire. He had just arrived with Murat.

Yusuf wanted more medicine for Dobbin from Istanbul, so I told him to go and find out how much it was and let me know before he bought it. He disappeared to Istanbul and rang the hotel two days later, saying he wanted £100.

I told him, 'Not on your life.' The following day a further message came: £50. I left a message with the receptionist that if he rang again, they were to tell him to come straight back and forget about the medicine. In the meantime, I exercised both the horses and treated Dobbin's dermatitis. It seemed to have stopped irritating him, but he had lost most of the hair on his head, neck and flanks and looked, superficially, worse than ever.

Three more days passed with no sign of Yusuf, so I rang the racecourse at Adana and asked if they would look after Dobbin and the cart for a couple of weeks, while I walked with Murat through the mountains. The manager kindly agreed. I hired a lorry and drove Dobbin and the cart to the railway station where, with the help of Ayhan, the lorry driver and the stationmaster, we managed, slowly, to coax both pony and cart up the station loading ramp and into the back of the lorry. Halfway down the southern face of the mountains, the driver halted and invited me for lunch at an open-air restaurant. We sat eating a huge pile of grilled lamb chops amid a horde of swirling hornets at which the laughing, cross-eyed cook swiped incessantly with a plank, putting his clientele at greater risk than the hornets. We reached the racecourse in the heat of the afternoon to find the smiling manager ensconced in the comfort of his air-conditioned office. Dobbin was assigned to a groom, with instructions to continue with the dermatitis treatment and to exercise him for at least half an hour every day, in the cart.

A comfortable air-conditioned bus delivered me back to Karaman at half-past four in the morning. Yusuf had returned that afternoon. He had spent the whole month doing, almost invariably, exactly what I had told him not to do, he was always surly and I could bear him no longer. After a violent row, in which he even threatened to run off with Murat, I paid him off with another month's salary and he departed. It was a distressing, horrible day, but once he had gone, it felt as if I had been freed from chains; a great load was lifted. I returned to the stables where Ayhan and I experimented with packing loads on the saddle for the start of the trek through the mountains the following morning.

IV

High Peaks and High Spirits

I left in the early morning, filled with elation at once more being on the move, and touched by Ayhan and his family, who crowded round me and pressed packets of cigarettes on me for the journey.

'May God protect you. Remember to write to us.' I promised I would. Some months later, I sent them a good photograph of their younger children.

A slight breeze tempered the heat as I walked away from the town, along a dusty earth road that wound its way slowly upwards through bare, burnt foothills, unrelieved by a single tree or bush. At first, Murat was difficult, being unused to carrying a pack, but he soon settled to the routine and in the early afternoon, I reached a village, perhaps a thousand feet above the level of the plain. In spite of the altitude, it was roasting hot; the surrounding mountains blocked the breeze and threw back the heat. A small stream ran down a narrow gulley, allowing a few tiny patches of cultivation to survive up its steep sides and tall poplars to grow out of the depths. I needed shelter for Murat until the cool of the evening and was offered the shady courtyard of a house that clung to the hillside. My elderly host's family were all out in the fields, a mile away, and as I rested, he brought me bread, cheese and grapes.

Both of us were slightly embarrassed; he by his obligations as a host without the support of his family and I because I did not wish to be in the way, but was unwilling to go any further until I could find a blacksmith, for Murat had cast a shoe en route. A neighbour was called in, both for advice and as an interpreter. He lived in Australia and had returned with his son for a holiday, and for the son to do his military service and find a wife. Both father and son spoke good English with strong Australian accents. The son had lived there most of his life, but he remained utterly Turkish; an Australian upbringing and education had changed neither Turkish customs nor loyalties.

'There's nobody here that can help, except one bloke that will shoe a horse occasionally, but he really only helps out the odd friend in emergencies and I think you want someone better than him. There is an old guy at Gölkaya, he's a blacksmith, old Bakkal Mehmet; he might be better,' said the father in broad Turkostrian.

'How far away is Gölkaya?' I asked.

'Only about half an hour or an hour away, over the back of the mountain there.'

So it was agreed that I would wait until five or six and then try Bakkal Mehmet (Mehmet the grocer). When the time came, it was to prove to be an hour and a half's walk, climbing up to and across another bare plateau and down into the adjoining gorge. I arrived at dusk, both of us tired and a little lame. I had aimed to start gently, walking only ten or twelve miles the first day but, in the end, found that I had walked over twenty.

Bakkal Mehmet, a rotund, bearded and busy fellow, had just returned from the hajj. He invited me in, fed and bedded me, but explained that he was off to Karaman on his motorbike first thing in the morning and did not have any horseshoe nails, so he could not help. When he left, I tethered Murat outside the forest guard's house for, with Mehmet away, I could not use his stable. I found a car going into Karaman, but it was Sunday and so there were no blacksmiths. I returned to the hotel and reread Robert Graves' short stories and played patience with my sticky, dirty patience cards to take my mind off my anxieties over Murat's lameness and my own carelessness at failing to check the shoes before I started. Yusuf obviously had not; he never did.

Monday morning brought Karaman to life and I found a blacksmith to come to Gölkaya for a pittance. We returned by taxi and, the shoeing completed, I set off slowly for Güldere, armed with a large handkerchief filled with bread, apples and plums, a contribution from Bakkal Mehmet's wife. The forest guard walked the first half-mile with me to set me on the right road. The track from Gölkaya to Güldere (Rose Rock to Rose Rill), led along a narrow gorge honeycombed with long, abandoned troglodyte dwellings in the cliffs. A clear stream, bordered by vegetable gardens and orchards of apples, plums and pears, ran beside it; willows and poplars lined the banks, and here and there were hedges, thickets of dog roses from which, perhaps, the valley had taken its name. Although it had been a late start, the day was cool, bright and glorious. In this little mountain paradise, I felt that only brown trout in the stream were lacking; maybe they were there, lurking among the tree roots in the stream, but if so I did not see them. But this was travel as it should be: a dream turned into reality.

The valley widened into the normal semi-desert for a mile or two before narrowing again into more terraced gardens and copses, and within two and a half hours, I had reached Güldere and camped in a plantation of poplars beside the stream. The village shop provided me with my few necessities and as I settled into my camp, the villagers came down to talk, bearing gifts of tea, bread and apples and cooking maize over twig fires. Laugher and chatter continued until long after dark. Murat's lameness had vanished, as had my anxieties with it, and an overwhelming happiness seemed to flow through my comfortably tired limbs. I fell asleep to the sounds of the water tumbling over the stones.

The morning was crisp as I took the path along the narrow gorge that led up from Güldere, deeper into the mountains. A mile out of the village, I met the only traffic I was to meet all day: a man and wife driving a pair of ponies in a hay cart, piled ten feet high with hay. The path plunged steeply, crossed a tiny bridge and rose equally abruptly on the other side of the little gorge. I stood aside to let them pass and watched, admiringly, as the man drove his pair at a trot down the precipitous slope, turned, deftly, over the bridge and started up the other side, a little exhibition of horse mastery. We exchanged friendly greetings as we passed and I climbed on for an hour or two over the next bare ridge and down into a broad valley beyond.

In spite of the altitude, it was hot again by mid-morning, so when I came to another small village, it was time to stop until the cool of the late afternoon.

A curious crowd collected around me as I tethered Murat and unloaded my possessions in the village square, through which pressed a very self-possessed fourteen-year-old girl who, addressing me in good English, announced, 'You must come to my house. Come and my mother will give you something to eat.'

Her father was the headmaster of a school in Mut, but it was now holiday time and the family had returned to their village to escape the heat and tend their beehives, for he was a keen beekeeper. Leaving me in their living room, listening to Vivaldi on a tape, mother and daughter began to prepare the meal. The music delighted me, even more so for being so wildly out of place and unexpected. I wondered what that seventeenth-century Venetian would have thought of his music being played in such a remote village of the Serene Republic's most implacable enemy. The only thing he would have understood would have been my means of transport.

Soon the father returned from his beehives. He described himself as merely an amateur apiarist, but the sale of the honey helped to subsidise his very small salary as a schoolteacher. After lunch, we were joined by a young cousin (an undergraduate, also with some English), and father, daughter, cousin and I walked down to his fields, a small and unproductive apple orchard and a stand of poplars. With two interpreters, conversation was easy. The daughter was another product of the excellent Anatolian High School system. He told me that the orchard merely provided fruit for the family, but the poplars were a substantial capital asset with a good market value when cut. In Anatolia and the Taurus, where timber is short, these small stands of fast-growing poplars are common and treasured. They provide a source of easily realised capital in case of emergencies.

As the afternoon began to cool, I set out again. My beekeeping friend had pointed out a mountain on the horizon.

'If you keep to the track that goes just to the right of that peak, it will eventually lead you to Civi, the next village,' he said. The additional height soon brought a cooling breeze, but it was four hours before I reached the top of the ridge and could just make out Civi, a dark smudge of trees in the valley beyond, that soon began to twinkle with an occasional light as night fell. I reached it a couple of hours after dusk and asked for the *muhtar* at the first house I reached. It was the *muhtar's* house I had chosen.

'Come in, come in.' he said. 'We will put your horse in my barn. Don't worry about fodder, I have plenty in there. *Mashallah*, you must be hungry.' A small, wiry man, his deeply lined face seemed a multiplication of smiles and within minutes I was seated in the middle of his family of wife and three handsome, merry daughters. We laughed and talked and teased over supper and for once my Turkish seemed to rise to the occasion. He then led me to the *kahveci* for a gossip with the rest of the village, but it had been a long day and when we returned and I was shown to a spare bedroom, I fell instantly into a dreamless sleep that lasted for nine hours.

The road from Civi followed another orchard-lined stream, for an hour or so, to Eleksi, where I was stopped by the locals for tea and a talk, so I tethered Murat to a bit of farm machinery. The name Eleksi was so unusual and unlike any Turkish name that I had ever met that I asked if anyone knew its origin. To me it sounded like a corruption of something Greek, a lost echo of Byzantium, but nobody could enlighten me. As we talked, Murat became bored, and pulling at his tether, upset the implement and in a moment of panic, started and broke his bridle, but a helpful farmer produced some saddler's tools and made a makeshift repair.

Thereafter the road rose steadily and relentlessly, and the stream and its line of green gave way to hot, bare rock and endless, dusty windings up the sides of an airless valley. Then, suddenly, I was on the top of the world: the watershed of the Taurus. A breeze dried the sweat of the climb and I stopped to stare. At 6,500 feet, the views were huge: range upon range of arid, empty mountains. In front of me, the now almost indefinable track led across a stony plateau; in the dips that retained a little soil, thin crops of barley or chickpeas had just been harvested and gusts of wind sent the dried chickpea bushes rolling across the landscape.

From one of these folds in the land, as out of nowhere, a young man appeared, riding a donkey.

'Why don't you ride?' he asked.

'With all my baggage, I would be too heavy for the pony – I would lame him,' I replied.

'But it is a fine horse, a strong horse. Go on and ride.'

But I had learned my lesson and kept walking. We went on our respective ways and in another hour, I had reached the first *yayla*, a nomad settlement of tents with rough drystone walls. It was bleak and waterless, although the good, broad track had allowed the nomads to tow up a large water cart and park it beside the tents for their daily needs.

By early afternoon, I had reached a more substantial settlement, Hac Pinar Yaylesi, a group of tents and rough stone huts beside a mountain stream, where the inhabitants invited me to stop and erect my tent. The surroundings were rocky and treeless, with only a few yards of green extending each side of the stream to soften the landscape. These semi-nomads told me that they came from Erdemli and spent two to three months every summer there to avoid the oppressive heat of the coast. It was remarkably well equipped, with a shop, a ramshackle affair of drystone walls, odd bits of timber and sheets of plastic for a roof, and a tented forecourt which acted as a *kahveci*. Away from the stream, they had dug communal privies and walled them with stone, and every couple of days a lorry came to restock the shop. The tents and stone shacks they made comfortable with carpets and cushions, but in a couple of weeks, they would be packing up and returning to the coast, for the winter starts early at that altitude and in a month or two, the place would be inaccessible under a six-foot blanket of snow.

These summer villages combine a holiday atmosphere with a normal working life: the barley, wheat and chickpeas are sown as soon as the snow goes and harvested in September; flocks of sheep and goats are driven up to graze the scant mountain herbage; and the women set up their looms beside the tents to weave more tents, saddlebags and mats. But half the present generation of nomads seem to go there purely for the pleasure of it, for the air and the freedom.

I pitched my tent a few yards from the stream and made it comfortable with my numnah for a mattress and saddle for a pillow, and because of the cold nights, sewed up a spare blanket to make a horse blanket for Murat, before joining the merry and welcoming crowd in the *kahveci*.

The night was cold, with my sleeping bag proving only just adequate, but the first hour of the next day's march soon warmed both horse and man. At midday, I was hailed by a nomad from Silifke and invited to tea and lunch and soon after, as the track began to lose height, the barrenness was relieved by ancient, gnarled cypresses and junipers, broken and twisted by the weight of the winter snows. By the evening, I had travelled twenty miles down to Mara, the old Armenian town whose name had so puzzled me in Karaman, and whose Turkification into Kırobası seemed to be steadfastly ignored by all the locals, even though the Armenians themselves had long since disappeared.

At two thousand feet below the level of the previous night, it is not a true *yayla*, for it is inhabited all the year round, although the summer population is double or treble that of midwinter. The shops were still open when I arrived and I headed for the saddler for some running repairs to saddle and bridle. I found him in his shop and was immediately invited to stay, as he had read about me in a local newspaper. A semi-nomad from Silifke, like many in the town, he had now settled to a more prosperous and bourgeois life with two saddlers' shops in Silifke and this one in Mara, to which he went every summer. However, this prosperity came with a bourgeois respectability which made the evening, for all his kindness, a little dull compared with the merry chatter of the *muhtar's* family at Civi or my friends in the *yayla* teahouse the night before.

I had covered some eighty miles in the last six days and Murat was tired and footsore, so I felt that a day's rest would do us both good. The following day was market day and the town soon filled with farmers, stalls and itinerant salesmen, and as I walked around the town, it became obvious that my arrival had added a bit of spice to the day's gossip.

I kept hearing whispers as I passed: '*O adam Istanbuldan bindi.*' (That man has ridden from Istanbul.)

With nothing to do, I climbed the small adjoining hill to the ruins of an Armenian castle. Little remained but ditches and foundations, but blocks of well-cut masonry were now incorporated into terrace walls on the slopes of the hill, a more productive use than that for which they had been hewn. I lunched in the only restaurant, then stretched myself out in the shade of an orchard and slept away most of the afternoon. I had stopped to rest Murat, but had discovered that I was equally weary. Nevertheless, I was unwilling to overstay my welcome, for the saddler had his sick father staying, a charming but very fragile old farmer, and I felt that I was imposing a burden on his wife. I asked about the next village, which was only a couple of hours' march away and, being given the name of a friend there, set out for Sarıaydın at half-past four.

The road climbed steeply, up among the junipers, and Murat moved unwillingly, needing to be coaxed and cajoled up the steeper stretches like a child, with little stops, soft words and a reassuring hand, until it plunged again into a gorge and down to the village. Houses lined the edge of the river, or grew like lichens out of the mountainside. Shouted enquiries to the *kahveci*, perched on a rock above the road, produced the saddler's friend, amazed and somewhat flattered that his name should be known to a *yabanci*, a stranger.

He led me to his house, newly built some three hundred feet above the valley, put a very tired Murat in a good, airy stable underneath the house and asked, 'Would you like a bath?' This was luxury beyond all expectations. There was no actual bath, but copious buckets of hot water were produced and I scrubbed myself from head to foot for the first time since leaving Karaman. My boisterous and enthusiastic host was a substantial, but illiterate, farmer of great generosity and high spirits. Neighbours came in for supper and a talk, and as at last they drifted off, bedrolls were taken from a large cupboard and spread on the living-room floor.

Murat appeared to have recovered in the morning but, for safety, I intended to make a short day of it. I was aiming for a village called Güzeloluk and had walked for

THE VERY
ENTHUSIASTIC
HUSEYIN

about three hours, up and down, up and down, through thin sprinklings of cypresses, junipers and cedars, when I met a lorry bumping along the dirt road, the first vehicle I had met for days. The driver stopped and addressed me in English.

'Where are you going?'

'To Güzeloluk.'

'Ask for Ahmet, the shopkeeper. He should be helpful. It is only about ten kilometres and I will meet you there for tea when I have delivered this load of flour.' He had learned his English when, as a soldier, some years before, he had been attached to the English section of the NATO headquarters in Izmir.

An hour later I passed through a small village, where I was greeted cheerfully by the shopkeepers and a farmer, who invited me to stay, but I had set my heart on Güzeloluk and so thanked him and carried on. Anyway, I had said I would meet the lorry driver there, but it proved to be a mistake. Güzeloluk, a word derived from 'beauty', did not live up to its name. It had no water and was surly. Ahmet, the shopkeeper, was not there, and when I asked about stabling and where I could put my tent, no helpful suggestion was forthcoming. I asked at the *kahveci* for the *muhtar* and, in reply, was only told that I must not tether Murat to the post at the corner of the building. For lack of anywhere else, I tied him to the bumper of a parked lorry, where he was pestered and teased by a group of tiresome children. After an hour or so the *muhtar* appeared and said that he did not think there was any stable or anywhere to pitch my tent, unless I pitched it beside the mosque. The place he indicated, a dozen yards from the *kahveci*, was cramped and filthy. The English-speaking lorry driver appeared, shrugged his shoulders, said he was sorry and drove off after joining me for a quick glass of tea.

At last, a teenager arrived, who said I could use his father's shed for 75p for the night, so we went to look at it. It was adequate. Having housed, groomed and fed Murat, I returned to the *kahveci* and the adjoining shop where I bought some bread and a watermelon; while eating them, an elderly and very poor nomad arrived and invited me to stay in his tent, a mile away. With my saddlebags over my shoulder, I followed him out of the town to a grove of trees, where his tent stood. He was recently widowed, he told me and lived with his daughter.

The daughter, a heavy and slovenly girl in her late teens or early twenties, greeted us and prepared some food and tea, at which we were joined, briefly, by a woman in her late forties, spare and slightly aggressive, who spoke mainly in curt grunts or growls.

'Don't worry about her,' explained the daughter, 'she is not quite right in the head.' But when we had eaten and settled down for the night, my host called out in a hoarse whisper to the woman to come back in, and from the subsequent grunting, it was apparent that he had found some solace in his widowhood.

Returning to the stable in the morning, I found that Murat had got at his fodder in the night and devoured the remaining five or six kilos of barley, but after a few hours of climbing back up through the juniper trees, he was again very tired, so we stopped in an abandoned *yayla*. I tied him to a pine tree, unearthed my camera and took a couple of photographs, but I was also tired, so I slept for an hour in the shade of the same tree. There was little or nothing for Murat to graze on and my own iron rations had gone bad after a week in the saddlebags, so I threw them out. But the place was beautiful, the views magnificent and the stillness of it broken only by little red squirrels scuttling in and out of the junipers.

For months, I had been so dogged by frustrations and disasters that I had reached the point of not wanting to look at the various horses in the morning when I woke, for fear of finding myself faced with some new catastrophe. Now, in these mountains, the ever-present anxieties dissolved; the daily journey of up to twenty miles was exhausting but a pleasure and the nightmares of failure had disappeared. Even the loneliness had gone, for human company seemed, for the moment, unnecessary, an intrusion on one's thoughts. Not that I did think deeply; I merely looked, admired and felt. I was filled with gratitude for the hospitality, for being here and for being alive, with an intensity that I had not known for years.

Mid-afternoon brought me down to a fertile valley and the *yayla* of Sorgun. A stream ran through the valley below the village for half a mile, until it tumbled in a series of waterfalls down a deep ravine and vanished among an impenetrable tangle of rocks. Where the stream began to fall, a watermill, powered by a ramshackle assembly of channels, pipes and cascades that would have defied even Heath Robinson's imagination, ground the village corn. The road followed the stream up the valley, between its fringe of poplars and plum and apple orchards, to the most substantial *yayla* that I had yet seen. Recent prosperity had converted it from a settlement of hair tents into a street of substantial single-storey houses, fronted by *kahvecis*, kebab stalls, grocers and greengrocers, hardware shops, a corn chandlery and a handsome new mosque. Yet it remained a true *yayla*, for in winter it was left to the care of a single village guard, holed up in the snow with half a year's supply of food and fuel.

I led Murat up the village street, bought him a supply of fodder and set up camp in an orchard beside the stream, where I was immediately surrounded by a crowd of inquisitive children, who had to look at everything that I possessed. But, unlike the children of Güzeloluk, their curiosity was well mannered and, with the aid of a packet or two of biscuits from the village shops, I found myself surrounded by willing helpers knocking in tent pegs, holding guy ropes, stowing away saddlebags and bedding and inundating me with a supply of apples. After half an hour of questions and answers, I escaped from my eager following to the *kahveci* for a glass or two of tea for, though in England I hardly drink a cup a month, in Turkey I had become addicted to it.

Here the questions and answers began all over again with a more adult audience, including the inevitable one in the mountains: 'Have you a map?' In these parts, a map does not mean a road map or a tourist map, or even an ordnance survey. Every villager is convinced that all visitors are really treasure-seekers in disguise and that they come with ancient maps showing where the treasure hordes are hidden in their mountains. This does not breed antipathy, for surely there will be enough gold for all if only we can find it, for everybody knows there were great, rich cities here in the olden days. Whose cities, of what great empire, they are not too sure, but they must certainly be there, waiting to be found. Any suggestion that their predecessors in the Taurus were unlikely to have been much more prosperous than themselves, and would certainly not flee without stuffing their coin of whatever realm in their trouser pockets before they did so, is inevitably greeted with scorn. Dreaming of treasure is an incurable and pleasing addition. It is also harmless.

'No, I have only a road map and as there are no roads here, there is nothing at all on the map except an occasional village, usually wrongly named.' But they never quite believed me.

As darkness fell the owner of the orchard invited me to a supper of the Turkish equivalent of baked beans, i.e. beans without the tin. The teenage daughter of the house was at college in Northern Cyprus and spoke a little incomprehensible English. For the next two hours, she tried very hard to convert me to Islam, until I found that, even with my broken Turkish, I could tease her. At this point, her father, a very poor but dignified old farmer, told her, with an indulgent smile, not to be so pestilential and the proselytising came to an abrupt end.

Murat needed a rest, so I stayed a day in that beautiful place, scrambling down the ravine as far as I could with one of the villagers, who pointed out strange little stretches of path, carved out of the rock face, that ended in nothing; of what era and for what purpose, neither of us could even guess. My guide then led me, breathlessly, up five hundred feet of mountainside above the gorge to the ruins of a castle, probably twelfth-century Armenian, perched on the crag above. Little remained beyond a couple of courses of well-cut granite masonry, but the views were breathtaking and the air like wine.

We returned to the village and a *kahveci*, where I was joined by a young undergraduate awaiting the results of his final examinations. He congratulated me on my Turkish, which was more than it deserved, but he had a fair command of English and so, with my dictionary on the table between us, we could carry on a broader conversation than I could normally manage. He was hoping for a post as a teacher following his results, but was doubtful as there were more graduates than available posts and in all events, he would have to do his military service first. Unlike so many national servicemen of my own era in England, he took his service not as a necessary but irritating chore that had to be performed, but as a personal duty and an obligation to the state, a return for the privilege of being Turkish. We talked of politics and he argued for a limited democracy in underdeveloped countries and for a more Islamic form of government for Turkey; he seemed to be seeking, both in his politics and his religion, the comfort, the security of certainties, of authority. Poor young man – though charming and interesting, he had yet found no certainties, was full of doubts and rather sad.

In the evening, the proselytising teenager again asked me in for tea and talk, but I had talked enough that day and wanted a bit of peace, so excused myself as politely as I could, with a promise to take photographs of her family in the morning, before I left.

The photographing delayed my departure, for the family all had to put on their best clothes, be lined up again and again, mother and daughter tried different ways of wrapping their shawls around their heads and the scruffy little brother was sent away to change into something cleaner, so my patience ran a little short. But my proselytiser was tyrannical.

'Just a few minutes more, just one more photograph.' I left with the pleadings still resounding in my ears and sent them, months afterwards, the most wooden of photographs, father, mother, daughter and son standing like carved statues, uncomfortable, unnatural and ill at ease.

The track was steep but passed through pleasant countryside, forever rising until I was again above the treeline amid the rocks and open, empty space. The path divided and divided again until, totally lost, I came to a substantial tent tucked into a fold of a mountain peak.

I was on the road, the nomads told me, not to Tarsus but to Mersin, but I must stay for lunch and then they would direct me back on the right track. The grey-bearded, portly father sat on a pile of cushions and beckoned me to join him, while his roguish son delved into his pocket to produce a seventeenth-century French silver coin, which he tried to sell to me for £10. It was in good condition and, although not in the least interested in buying it, I was fascinated as to how it could have found its way into the mountains. Had it fallen from some French traveller's pocket, or was all silver acceptable as currency here at some time in the past and traded indiscriminately along the coast? There was no answer. A handsome and statuesque daughter brought in the meal with lithe, swinging movements and I tried not to look too admiringly at her, which was difficult, for she was a beautiful creature. Her brother reduced the price of the coin to £5, but I told him to take it down to Mersin and sell it to a tourist for at least £10 or £15; it was worth it. Years later, I was to learn about the French and English Levant companies trading out of Izmir and Aleppo; the French were permitted to export specie to pay for the import of silks but the English were not – they had to export goods, principally English cloth – so this Louis III or Louis IV coin must have fallen off the back of some Armenian merchant's donkey here in the Taurus, three hundred years ago.

Food was followed by the visit of the pompous *muhtar*. A pop-eyed and stupid man, he marched into the tent and, without a greeting, demanded, 'Why have you come here? Who permitted it?'

'I came here because I was lost, and I need no permission. The Turkish government is aware of my journey.'

He subsided slightly but not much, keen to impress me with his importance. 'Are you looking for gold?' The old treasure-hunting bit again.

'No, I am looking for the road to Arslanköy.'

'It's back the way you came.'

'I have already discovered that.'

He left as abruptly as he had come, obviously piqued that foreigners should be allowed to travel in his bailiwick, and even more so that they should not be in awe of his great authority.

After he had gone, my host made deprecating noises about his manners (he was obviously not a popular appointment), and I started back along the track on which I had come.

'Keep to the right at the spring,' the son told me, and made a final half-hearted attempt to sell his coin. But I found no spring, and towards dusk, camped by a stream near a couple of tents that I had already passed early that morning, and whose occupants, with the usual generosity of the mountains, invited me in for supper.

As I was packing up my tent in the morning, a child came down from the tents up the hill, carrying a kettle of tea, and bread and cheese for my breakfast. I set off in search of the spring, but never found it; it was three hours before I was at last directed, by a lone traveller, onto the right track, and a further hour and a half before it tipped over the edge of the barren plateau and sank into a widening green valley of a beauty unsurpassed by any that I had yet seen.

As I paused on a little rise at the head of the valley, staring, entranced, at the view, a very European figure appeared half a mile below, marching sturdily up the road towards me. We stopped to pass the time of day. He was a young Swiss whose wife was teaching German at Sivas, and he was taking a break for a week, walking through the mountains. He asked me about a nearby lake, but it did not appear on my map so I was unable to help and we went our separate ways.

The valley was enchanting, filled with apple, plum and peach orchards dissected by running streams. Over damp patches in the road, hosts of blue and yellow butterflies hovered, little kaleidoscopic clouds of living, moving colours. A farmer halted me by an orchard gate and filled – overfilled – my pockets and saddlebags with delicious plums and peaches which, tired and hungry as I was, were very welcome. I walked on down, munching and sharing my feast with Murat, plum by plum, peach by peach.

I reached the village of Arslanköy at one, after five hours of walking, to find a good and welcoming restaurant and a place for Murat in a neighbouring yard. The owner invited me to camp in the garden behind, where my tent was pitched with the dubious help of half a dozen eager small boys whom I rewarded with bars of chocolate from a nearby shop. The restaurant produced some hot water for my first shave for a couple of days; my first cigarette for a day or two filled me with satisfaction; the raki with my supper that evening, after two weeks of abstinence, was nectar, and a superb melon ambrosial. All that was missing was somebody with whom to share the pleasures and exultation, in a tongue that I could command. But that was a minor diminution of paradise. I extracted some crumpled paper and envelopes from a saddlebag and tried to express it in letters to England, while sitting in the shade of the restaurant garden. The views across the wide and fertile valley and the friendliness of all about me added to my euphoria, but I doubt if my letters did it justice; euphoria is not easy to define in words.

Murat again needed a rest, so I stopped for another day. At lunch, a farmer joined me and, in his enthusiasm, filled and refilled our raki glasses and insisted that I should come to his house and look at some strange caves, carved out of the boulders halfway up the adjoining mountainside. With his son and young cousins, we climbed, panting, up the mountain, and on our return, were welcomed with another gargantuan meal and more raki, which I resisted as best as I could, but politeness required that I should drink at least another glass or two.

In the middle of it all, the Swiss arrived, walking down the hill we had just climbed and joined the party. Although his Turkish was infinitely superior to mine, he was a heavy and over-earnest young man whose spirit did not appear to take wings either from alcohol or from the beauty of the place, so when he moved on into the village in search of a lift down to the coast, there was a slight but general sense of relief. At dusk, my host insisted that I should stay the night, and when the food and drink were finally removed, a bedroll was laid for me on the living-room floor.

The merry disorders of the day before brought the usual penalties in the morning. We rose early, but all my possessions and Murat were a mile away at the other end of the village, and progress was slow. In packing up my camp and loading Murat, I lost my iron tethering stake and had to wait for an hour until I could find a blacksmith to make me another. Each blow on the anvil reverberated through me from head to toe and I was glad to get on the road, where I could walk off the effects of my overindulgence without being required to make conversation.

The road was a real one with an asphalt surface, the first since I had left Karaman, and started in great beauty with wisps of cloud hanging about the high-lit peaks. It descended through more and more peach orchards, full of villagers harvesting the fruit, then rose again into tracts of monotonous pine forest where, on the steep inclines, Murat found the tarmac slippery and difficult. At midday I stopped briefly at a village to buy fruit and more fodder, then carried on steadily downwards, walking without thought through more barren, maquis-covered hills until, suddenly, a shot rang out a few yards from me. Startled, Murat gave an involuntary kick and his iron shoe caught me on the point of the heel.

It was only a local sportsman firing at a partridge, but the kick was a painful one and for the next five or ten minutes I could not walk. As the initial shock faded, I started out again, somewhat lamely, and walked for a further two hours to Bekiralanı, the next village along the road. I tied Murat to a telegraph pole, sank gratefully onto a chair in the *kahveci* and asked where I could find a stable. That day I had walked for eight hours and covered twenty-five miles.

Within a few minutes a small, rotund haji arrived and invited me to stay. Haji Seref was in his late thirties, a prosperous small farmer. We walked to his house and stabled Murat in the cowshed beneath it. He led me

127

upstairs to meet his wife and daughters, all little, round, smiling people, like carbon copies of himself.

'Would you like a shower? Shall we take and wash your clothes?' All the little, round people bustled about me, thinking of every possible thing for my comfort.

'This is better than a five-star hotel,' I joked, and provoked happy giggles and tut-tuts from the band of bustlers. Once scrubbed and cleanly clad, I was set in front of an excellent supper and when that was over, neighbours trooped in to talk, including a pleasant English-speaking girl.

The advantage of having a translator, when one is tired, is enormous. The perpetual strain of keeping up a conversation in an unfamiliar language is exhausting; if one is too tired to try and allows the mental shutters to fall, it looks like surliness, which is a poor return for the villagers' inexhaustible kindnesses. My interpreter was a graduate working in Ankara, who had returned to the village for her holidays. Although originating from the village, she now found the restrictions of village life difficult. Nobody, among her local friends, could understand her, an unmarried woman in her mid-twenties, being unwilling to give up her city life for a village husband and the intellectual limitations that such a choice would impose. To a villager, it was incomprehensible. In a man, such an ambition and a city life would seem like progress, a thing to be proud of, but in a woman it was just odd, an unreasonable quirkiness. The gulf between metropolis and village, between the Westernised life and the traditional, is enormous and full of incomprehension. The visitors did not stay late but, in spite of my weariness, I slept little that night, for my heel gave me streaks of pain each time I moved.

In the morning, Haji Seref and I walked down to the *kahveci*, perhaps two hundred yards away, but I was so lame, I could only just make it. It was impossible for me to travel any further for at least a day. After watching Murat's feet with such care for the past two weeks, it was my heel that brought me to a halt. I was extremely embarrassed. Such was the kindness I had received that I was unwilling to impose myself on Seref and his family for another day, but I had little option. They were totally unperturbed.

'Poor fellow, of course you can stay, stay as long as you need.' After half an hour at the *kahveci*, we returned to the house and I slept for three hours, having to be woken for lunch. Seref was the most attentive of hosts, bathing my injured foot, bringing me my lunch on a tray and returning every few minutes to my room to see if there was anything that I needed. Later I got up again and joined the women of the household in the living room, six little knitting people knitting six jerseys, while watching an American film on the television. It was, of course, dubbed in Turkish, so I could not understand a word of it.

By dawn, my heel was sufficiently improved to try again and I left early, seen off by the entire smiling family with a chorus of 'Go with smiles, good luck. Write when you get to Jerusalem.' When I did get there, they were among the first people I wrote to. I hobbled slowly down the road through valleys filled with peach and grape pickers. At this lower altitude, the villages were more frequent and there was some traffic again on the roads. As I walked, a car stopped and the driver got out and addressed me in broken English.

'Where are you from and where are you going?'

I told him.

'*Mashallah*! You must stay tonight at my house. I will not be there, but here are the keys.' Here was the ultimate trust and hospitality, but the house was in a village off my route and I was embarrassed by this extraordinary kindness. I explained my route and why I must refuse his offer.

'Then you will go by Burhan, and I have a friend there.' He wrote the name and address on a piece of paper. 'I am only half a good man, but he is a very good man and rich too.' Pressing both the piece of paper and a good ball pen into my hand, he jumped back into his car and sped off. But sadly I did not get as far as Burhan that night, for I would have liked to have met the 'very good man'. As far as I could see, the place abounded with them.

At four o'clock, I reached a small, poor village clustered around the ruins of yet another Armenian castle. Stopping a man on a tractor, I asked if I could buy some fodder and if there was somewhere that I could stable or tether Murat.

'Stay with me,' he said. 'There is no fodder here, but I will be back. Wait here.' I waited for an hour and a half and when there was still no sign of him, I went in search of the *muhtar*.

I found him, a taciturn man, who told me to tether

Murat in his tractor shed. Fortunately, I had enough fodder for the evening, for it was a fruit-growing area and neither barley nor chopped straw were readily available. The *muhtar* was obviously a very successful farmer and had a wider understanding of the world than most of the mountain people that I had met, but his broader education had not equipped him to deal with women. Already once divorced, he was clearly a bad picker or a plain bad husband, for his wife argued and complained all the time I was there. Soon, he decided we would go to Mersin, twelve miles away, for a drink, so we jumped into his pickup and drove to a cafe on the waterfront. Over the drink we sat almost in silence as the extraneous musical din pouring out of some loudspeakers made conversation impossible. An acquaintance, slightly seedy and obviously a well-known toper, joined us at the table and appeared to be trying to extract both a free drink and some other favour as well, but when his glass was not replenished after the first drink, he sloped off to try his luck elsewhere.

We drove back into the centre of the town for supper at a restaurant, for which I managed to pay, but even in the relative quiet of the restaurant, I could extract little conversation, except about the price of oranges, the extent of his orange groves and the burden of his tasks as *muhtar*. I began to have some sympathy for his wife, for he was not an easy man. On our return, I laid out my sleeping bag on his balcony and when I awoke at half past six in the morning, he had already left for his fields. I was not sorry.

The first village was two hours away and proved also

to have no fodder for Murat, so I plodded on to the next, a further two hours in increasing heat, for I had left the mountains behind and was back on the coastal plain. The village seemed dead: neither the shops nor the *kahveci* were open, and the streets were empty. However, a woman in a doorway told me she could sell me some barley. The shops, she said, would be open in an hour or so, so I carried the barley back to the *kahveci* where I had tethered Murat and sat down on the veranda, watching him eat. By now the temperature was approaching 100° and I had acquired a crop of blisters to add to my bruised and still very painful heel. A peasant woman joined me and we talked. Her face was a tapestry of deep wrinkles and smiles, but she was a formidable lady, which was perhaps why she was the only woman I ever met in a *kahveci*, an otherwise exclusively male preserve; her strength of character clearly matched or overpowered that of the village menfolk. After questioning me about my travels, she told me that Tarsus was still eight miles away, but I would find a *han* for Murat in the centre of the town.

At last the *kahveci* opened and produced me some lunch and I limped on again, arriving in Tarsus at dusk, riding in the back of a cart, whose driver gave me a lift for the last mile to the *han*, with Murat tied to the tailboard.

I can understand St Paul's travellings. There is not a lot to hold one in Tarsus today and I suspect it was not much more exciting in his day, although then it was a port, before the alluvial silt pushed out the coastline and silted up the river. It is just one of those dull places where things happen by pure chance, without the place itself having any relation to the happening or the consequences, like battlefields. St Paul was born there, Antony and Cleopatra met there, so it manoeuvres itself into the pages of the history books and we all know about it, without anything else to justify its fame.

It was even the place of a happening on the First Crusade. Two of the princes, the Apulian Norman Tancred and Baldwin of Boulogne, captured it, without even a battle, from a small Turkish garrison and then fell out over who should hold it. In the resulting dispute, Baldwin shut out three hundred Norman infantry who were slaughtered by the fleeing Turks in the night, an act of callous selfishness and greed that affected the relations between the two long after they had abandoned the town on the grounds that it provided them with no profit, and they had become, respectively, the Prince of Antioch and the King of Jerusalem.

I was held there for a day by sore feet. The road from Tarsus to Adana is a dull, flat highway filled with heavy traffic and the resultant diesel fumes. Murat and I plodded very slowly along the twenty-mile stretch, stopping occasionally for food or drink, until we came to a sign on the front of a factory announcing that it was the Lee Cooper jeans factory. One of my two pairs of moleskin trousers was already torn and badly patched up to keep me decent, but both were much too heavy for the steamy Cilican plain. In advertisements, jeans always seem to adorn cowboys in very macho poses, set against a background of great open spaces, but it must have been the first time in Turkey that a cowboy had ever tied his horse to the front of a jeans factory and walked in to buy a pair. The girl behind the counter in the factory shop was quite unmoved. She served me the ritual glass of tea, found a couple of pairs that looked as if they would fit, ushered me into the fitting room to try them and returned to reading her newspaper. Only I seemed to find the situation odd. I bought a pair, stowed them in a saddlebag and departed.

The last five or six miles seemed a perpetuity; I expected the Adana racecourse to appear at each of the rare bends on that hot, straight road, but it did not until I had been travelling for nine hours. When I saw it, the relief was enormous. As I stumbled down the last hundred yards to the racecourse stable, a groom relieved me of Murat, another brought out a chair and a third produced yet more glasses of reviving tea. The cart stood where I had last seen it three weeks before, and Dobbin, I was informed, had completely recovered. In the meantime, Murat and I had walked two hundred miles.

V

Armenian Kings and Crusader Princes

The heat and humidity of Adana brought down on me the accumulated tiredness of the last two weeks. It came as something of a surprise. Such had been the elation of walking through the Taurus that I had not been aware of my underlying weariness; except for the last day or so, after the kick on my heel, I had been able to outwalk Murat most of the time and had considered myself indestructible.

Thus, to find myself now, back in civilisation, unable to think and devoid of willpower, was frustrating. I rang a Turkish friend of a friend on arrival and went to dinner with him that evening, still buoyed up by the excitement, but the following day, I found that what Turkish I had, had disappeared. All I could achieve in the day was to draw some money from the bank before sinking onto my bed to read Hemingway's *Farewell to Arms*, which I found in another English-language bookshop; I had last read it twenty-five years before.

In the evening, I emerged from my hotel room and went out for dinner at the best hotel in the town. At the adjoining table sat another lone stranger and we began to talk. He was an Italian of great charm; born in Istanbul, he had returned to Turin some years before, breaking thereby a family connection of six hundred years with Turkey, the last of a long line of merchant adventurers. I wished afterwards that I had had the energy to question him further on his family. What chance or feud at home could have led them to settle, at the end of the fourteenth century, in Constantinople? How did they survive the Ottoman conquest of the city half a century later, or did the Italian communities, across the Golden Horn at Galata, survive untouched? What trade was it that enabled them to continue to prosper, generation after generation? It would be a fascinating story, if only it could be told. But I was too tired to ask the questions and he was returning home the following day.

My lethargy lasted for forty-eight hours. Then, as I had decided, with Dobbin fit again, to drive a pair of horses from here on, I needed to find someone who could make the rubber-lined shoes necessary for roadwork, buy the additional harness and alter the cart to accommodate the change. I returned to the stables to find Dobbin well, but as in Istanbul, the groom had totally ignored my instructions to exercise him in the cart, so his actual fitness was in doubt. Also, as I had never driven a pair and knew nothing about the harness, I needed help.

As I helped the groom wash down the horses, another fat but cheerful fellow sat making caustic comments from a nearby bench, but then offered to come with me to the saddler and blacksmith in the town. He had been

a jockey and, having become too heavy, had driven his own phaeton around his hometown of Ceyhan until the local authority introduced a ban on horse transport, forcing him back to the stables as a groom. His name was Huseyin. We harnessed Murat; the first time I had put him in the cart. Huseyin drove him off at a reckless pace around the edges of the town to try him out, while I went in search of new shoes for both the horses, armed with sketches of their feet drawn on an old newspaper. I returned later, having been promised the shoes the following day, to find Huseyin and a friend cantering back down the track to the stables, singling lustily and waving bottles of beer. There were a number of empties already rolling about the bottom of the cart, but Murat was declared a success. It was quite clear that Huseyin and his pal's party was equally successful.

The following day, surprisingly, did produce the shoes on time and the Jockey Club blacksmith agreed to fit them. He told me that these shoes, the *lastik nalleri*, had originated with the Russian army, but how or when they had been adopted by the Turks, I could not ascertain. We then harnessed Dobbin and set off, at the same wild speed, for the saddler and the cart maker on the far side of the town, returning late in the evening with all the tasks performed. The cart had acquired a new load of empty beer bottles, as well as a large, jumbled heap of assorted harnesses. Adana is a modern commercial town and filled with traffic, so perhaps Huseyin had something; driving a horse and cart through the midst of it, in rush hour, is less unnerving after a few bottles of beer. It also softened the shock of being almost £200 poorer.

Huseyin had begun to take me in hand and organise me, whether I liked it or not. On the whole, I did. The following day, he offered his services to travel with me as far as the Syrian border and we agreed a not inconsiderable fee, in Turkish terms. He then enrolled his drinking pal of the previous day to help him harness the pair and, dismissing me as an unnecessary encumbrance for the moment, sent me back to the hotel while he tried out the two together.

It was to prove a satisfactory arrangement. Short and stocky, like most Turks, his enjoyment of his beer had given him, in his mid-thirties, a substantial beer-drinker's gut. He was extraordinarily meticulous – every knot I tied was checked and retied, the harness had to be exactly fitted according to his scheme of things, the baggage loaded and secured just so – but it worked. His only major failing was overenthusiasm. But he was good, entertaining company.

The day we planned to set out, it was still very hot, so we waited until five o'clock in the afternoon before driving my 'carriage and pair' back to the saddler for final adjustments to the harness. By eight, we had reached Incerlik, a village five miles out of Adana, and drew up outside a smart roadside restaurant for something to eat. As the village adjoins a US air force base, it was crowded with American air force personnel and the quality of the menu, if not the prices, was high.

But tethering a cart and pair of horses in a car park presents problems: cars do not, on a flat piece of ground, go wandering off about their own mysterious business.

Horses do. Thus, our drinks and the meal were frequently interrupted by shouts and Huseyin dashing away from the table to secure our errant transport. Eventually, we took a spare shaft from the back of the cart and passed it through the spokes of the back wheels, a technique I was to use for the rest of the journey. The American airmen and their families in the restaurant were already suffering from culture shock in Turkey and thus they thought that going out to dinner with a horse and cart was just another part of Turkish daily life, a quaint local custom. So they did the only thing they could: they politely ignored it.

Well fed and revived, we took to the road again. We soon turned off onto a quieter side road and drove through a deepening but starlit darkness, illuminated only by pricks of light from distant villages and the occasional spark from the horses' hooves. When we reached the old arched bridge at Misis, the moon had risen and cast a wobbling line of gold on the water, but the romance of it vanished as we drew up and camped on the village football pitch and lay down to sleep, tentless, at midnight. Dawn showed that the field was also used as the village rubbish tip.

When I awoke at half-past five, Huseyin had already fed and watered the horses. There was a heavy dew and the air was very cool until the sun rose above the ridge of hills to the east. After an hour, we could see Yılan Kalesi, the Snake Castle, one of the most dramatic of all the Armenian castles, emerging from the mist that rose up around the isolated crag it crowns. Its history has long vanished in the tumultuous ebb and flow of invading races but, if seen at dawn, the imagination can create its own stories. We stopped for tea in the village at the foot of the crag and I took some photographs that were never to be developed.

By ten, we reached Ceyhan, Huseyin's hometown, where he left me for an hour to deliver part of his pay to his parents, with promises that he would find a stable and that we must stop with his family. After two hours, he returned. His parents were away and there was no place for the horses. It was getting hot again and, having been left on a piece of wasteland in the sun, my temper was getting short. We had also already covered nearly forty miles since we had set out and I was worried about the state of the horses but, as there appeared to be no alternative, we moved on.

We drove on and on through the afternoon, through the belt of stony hills that rise a few hundred feet to divide the plain from the coast, past small patches of shrivelling, under-watered cotton and occasional fields of more thriving vines. As we crawled slowly up the street of a small village, we were met with a great yell of triumph and a crowd pouring excitedly out of the *kahveci*. Turkey had just won an Olympic gold medal. We stopped and joined the crowd, who ran back to the television to watch what was to be the first of a thousand reruns of the film sequence that would continue until I crossed the border into Syria. But there was still nowhere to camp, so we dragged on over the crest of the hills to the sea and an abandoned holiday camp on Iskenderun Bay.

Unharnessing the exhausted horses by the beach, we discovered that the camp was not completely empty.

Three farmers from near Ceyhan had remained behind for a little quiet fishing, now that their wives had taken their children back home for the beginning of the school term. One of them knew Huseyin and invited us to join them for supper. We contributed some cash and one the farmers mounted his motorbike and disappeared to the nearest village for a supply of raki and beer, while Huseyin and I led the horses into the sea to rinse off the day's sweat and dust. A small wooden bridge crossed a stream and beyond it the farmers occupied a couple of primitive but comfortable huts, and we dined on fish fresh from the stream, washed down with the raki and beer. A few glasses seemed to lubricate my Turkish, which became quite fluent, but when we returned to our tents to sleep, Dobbin was lying down and did not look well.

Huseyin's enthusiasm had produced its first casualty; he had grossly overestimated Dobbin's state of fitness after six weeks without work and the gruelling first twenty-four hours had left him very lame. There was no alternative but to sell the poor fellow and find a replacement. With Murat alone in the shafts and Dobbin trailing behind, we set off for Dörtyol, the Issus of Alexander's defeat of Darius. Back on the main highway, we found a restaurant where we could rest the horses for the heat of the day under some trees and with an ample supply of water from irrigation channels, an opportunity the meticulous Huseyin could not waste; within minutes, he was stripped to his underpants and scrubbing every spare article of clothing he possessed. After lunch, we hailed an empty lorry and I hired it to take Dobbin the last ten miles to Dörtyol, leaving Huseyin to follow on with the cart. He arrived later, cursing, for while we had been lunching, someone had rifled the cart and stolen some of his newly scrubbed clothes.

His family had friends in Dörtyol. A very poor family of carters, they had fallen on hard times since the death of the father, a Turk from Palestine, who had migrated there in the upheavals that followed the First World War and had set up as a porter. He had become a famous local strongman and had prospered, buying first a horse and cart and then a little land. With pride, his son, Tahsin, related the tale of how, in his youth, his father had been given a prize of some money by Atatürk himself, for running up a local mountain under an enormous load. His frail little widow had been born in Salonika, where Atatürk had been a neighbour, but was too young to remember him. The great man was already a figure in the world, she told me, when she was born.

Tahsin, a gentle soul like his mother, obviously lacked the drive and acumen of his father, but helped us find a horse to replace Dobbin in the morning. It looked healthy enough and had, we were informed, come from Iskenderun the day before. We harnessed the pair and trotted slowly along the dull coast road for the last twenty miles to Iskenderun, where the only *han* was so unhelpful that we had to put the animals in a garden at the edge of the town before I settled myself in a comfortable, old-fashioned hotel on the seafront.

In spite of its foundation by Alexander, Iskenderun is a modern town; it is not even very Turkish, which is not surprising in view of its polyglot population and the fact that it was only reincorporated into modern Turkey as late as 1939. The population speaks Arabic almost as freely as Turkish and still includes a substantial Christian minority, a rarity in Turkey after the exodus of the Greeks and the Armenians. It could be lifted up bodily and placed almost anywhere in the eastern Mediterranean, yet not look or feel out of place. The seafront architecture and palms could even fit in Spain or southern Italy. I found a pleasant Dutch couple, with almost immaculate English, in the hotel dining room, whom I joined for drinks and supper. A good supply of wine and their own bottle of brandy enabled us to solve most of the world's problems, philosophical and economic, with surprising ease.

Huseyin joined me for breakfast with an expression of mixed anxiety and rage. The new horse was as lame as Dobbin after only twenty miles. His self-esteem and his reputation, he felt, were both diminished. But you cannot buy a Bucephalus for only a hundred pounds, even at Issus.

'We must go back to Dörtyol and find that liar, that cheating horse dealer. He is not an honourable man, it is shaming...' I have never found a horse dealer who *was* an honourable man and expected no profitable result from going back there, but Huseyin needed to let fly at someone, to relieve his feelings. In the event, the horse dealer, like all sensible horse dealers, had vanished and it was poor Tahsin who received the brunt of his wrath. While Huseyin stormed through the town, roaring threats of the wildest nature, I pottered around trying to see exactly where the great Battle of Issus had taken place, but could not make it out at all. Reading Robin Lane Fox's biography of Alexander again, much later, I found that it was probably some miles south of Dörtyol where the coastal strip is much narrower, so my incomprehension was hardly surprising. At four o'clock I decided that I had better go back and feed the horses and leave Huseyin to fume at all who came within range.

He returned at supper time to say that he had found a replacement. I looked at the new pony in the morning; it was a minute, underfed, scarred creature with a sad face.

'That?' I asked in horror. 'That will get us nowhere. It is a walking disaster, a pile of bones, a nothing.'

'It is fit and has been trotting every day around the town for years in a phaeton,' Huseyin claimed. 'And it is cheap.'

'How cheap?'

'Only a hundred pounds and we don't pay anything if it falls sick before we get to Antakya.'

With a snort of disgust, I went off to catch a bus to the frontier post on the road to Latakia, to look at the road and to enquire, at the customs post, what documentation I would need to take the horses and cart across the frontier. The road rose steeply, very steeply, behind Iskenderun to the pass through the Amanus Mountains, the Syrian Gates, and then dropped down the far side to the broad, open Orontes Valley leading to Antakya. The bus stopped there and I had to take a taxi on the last thirty miles to the frontier post. The road was steep and winding and would be very difficult with the cart. As I talked to the taxi driver, in a mixture of Turkish and Arabic, I questioned him about the road thereafter.

'Do you know it?'

'Yes, it is all like this until the last few kilometres to Latakia.'

'What about fodder for the horses, is it as easy to find there as here?'

'No problem,' he replied.

When asked about the documentation necessary to take the horses through to Syria, the smiling customs man at the frontier post was very helpful.

'I don't know, we do not have carts crossing the frontier, but I don't think you need any documentation on this side at all, but on the other, they will probably want a veterinary certificate.'

'Where do I get that?'

'At the Ministry of Agriculture offices either in Iskenderun or Antakya.'

I thanked him for his help and returned, by taxi and bus, to Iskenderun. I had told Huseyin that I would be back at around one, but did not arrive until two. There was no sign of him, the cart or the horses, so I returned to the hotel. The telephone in my room rang at four.

'It's Huseyin. I am in Belen, come straight away; the new horse is pure gold.'

I packed up quickly in the hotel, paid my bill and grabbed a taxi for Belen, halfway up the mountain to the Syrian Gates. Huseyin was waiting. There had been a shower of rain after I had left and he had taken advantage of the cool to start up the mountain and was very excited by how the pair had worked. As we started up on that very difficult road, he was full of praise for the new horse.

'If Murat is silver, it is gold, pure gold,' he kept repeating. 'It does not stop for anything.' It was certainly pulling extremely well and he had to keep flicking Murat with the whip to stop him shirking and leaving all the work to the other. We climbed for another hour and reached the top of the pass as darkness fell. I had enjoyed our night drive a few days earlier, but this was a different matter; then we had been on an unsurfaced road devoid of traffic and on a dead flat plain, but now we were on the steepest road I had ever driven on and it was the main trunk road to Syria. Heavy lorries ground up and down in low gear and the night was black and moonless. The new pony had to be restrained from breaking into a canter, while Murat anxiously held back, nervous of slipping on the smooth tarmac.

Huseyin drove, with great skill, while I shone a torch backwards and forwards to alert the passing traffic. We tried to hang a hurricane lamp from the canopy frame to make us a little more obvious in the darkness, but it made little difference and banged against the backs of our heads, so we abandoned the idea. After two more hours, we reached the foot of the mountain and pulled, with relief, into a petrol station. Huseyin was unmoved, but I had found the drive hair-raising. But the petrol station had, surprisingly for one on such a major junction, neither a restaurant nor even a *kahveci*. Having settled down the horses and consigned them to the temporary care of the pump attendants, we caught a minibus to the nearest small town, only five miles away, for a meal. When we had eaten, Huseyin suggested, out of kindness, that he should return to the cart, while I slept the night in a hotel in the town. He, however, had the best of the bargain: the hotel was airless, dirty and hot, with a supply of a thousand mosquitoes for each guest. At three o'clock, to relieve the irritation of the mosquito bites and to cool myself, I took a cold shower, but managed to get a couple of hours' sleep thereafter.

I was back at the cart by six and we were off soon after, only to find that Murat had lost half a shoe, so we crept very slowly to the next village in search of a blacksmith. There was, we were told, no blacksmith before Antakya, so we did our best with a spare horseshoe nail to secure the remaining half and continued, cautiously, on our way.

With this shoe problem, I was forced to abandon a plan I had to visit Baghras, the most northerly crusader castle captured by Saladin, although he dismantled and abandoned it a few years later when threatened by the German armies of the Third Crusade. After the Battle of Hattin in 1187, when he destroyed almost the entire chivalry of the crusading states in a single day, Saladin's army devoted itself to the recovery of Jerusalem and the reduction of all the crusader strongholds that it could. A few were too strong to attempt; some of the others resisted, with despairing courage, up to a year of siege; but most fell like ripe apples. The garrisons that should have defended them and the armies that might have come to their relief were either dead on the shores of the Sea of Galilee, prisoners awaiting ransom, or slaves already dispersed around the Islamic world.

Baghras lies a mile or two off the main road, on a prominence among the foothills of the Amanus range, and the old road over the pass we had crossed in the night used to run just below it. I had first visited it some seven years earlier and photographed it on a hot September day, struggling over the ruins and the surrounding hills with a heavy bag full of cameras and spare lenses, until the sweat ran so profusely down my face and into my eyes that I could not see to carry on.

It is a grim place: originally built by the Byzantines to check the Arab raids across the pass into Cilicia, it was the source of bitter disputes and intrigues between the Armenians, the Knights Templar and the crusader Princes of Antioch. It was the cause of battles, treacheries, kidnappings and blackmail of princes, and even an intervention by the Pope, who threatened to excommunicate King Leo II of Armenia if he did not return it to the Templars, a fate that the wily old monarch ignored; the Armenian Church's recognition of papal supremacy was skin-deep and did not include allowing popes to give away kings' castles. We trotted on, past the turning to Baghras, up the broad Orontes Valley until, in the late afternoon, we reached Antakya, put the cart and horses in a *han* and collapsed, gratefully, in the relative comfort of the nearest hotel.

Antakya, or Antioch, like İznik, has an illustrious past, but very little today to show for it. Time, geology and politics have been equally unkind. Founded in 300 BC, by a successor to part of Alexander the Great's empire, it grew to be the principle city of the Roman Empire in the east, a city renowned for its luxury, its trade with the east and its licence. St Peter founded the first Christian church in a cave there, and its crusader Gothic facade remains. There are still notices, in a collection of languages, telling those good Christian pilgrims who visit it that the journey entitles them to a plenary indulgence, if carried out with due zeal and humility. But Antioch's history includes more zeal than humility, and the licence, centred on the adjoining Temple of Apollo at Daphne, permeated the spirit of successive generations.

As a border stronghold between east and west, it was forever changing hands; the Persians sacked it in 540 AD, recaptured it and held it for a few years in the seventh century; the Byzantine Emperors recovered it and lost it again, almost immediately, to new invaders, the Arabs, who were to hold it for the next three hundred years; until a later emperor revived the imperial arms and for a further hundred years it was again a Byzantine city until betrayed to the Turks by its disaffected and renegade governor.

The crusaders arrived at its gates in the autumn of 1097 and although their impetus and reputation were such that they would have been unlikely to resist an immediate and determined assault, the sheer size of the walls and the town itself cowed them. After months crossing Asia Minor, they were exhausted; the princes were already distrusting the ambitions of their colleagues and lacked the joint will for so desperate a venture. They decided on a siege, and for the next six months, almost starved to death around its walls.

Winter brought incessant rain and famine, and

despair increased the desertions, including Stephen of Blois, William the Conqueror's son-in-law. Roused from their lassitude by necessity, they defeated two relieving Turkish armies, but when, by treachery, they gained entry to a tower by night and flooded in to sack the city, they were immediately besieged themselves by the largest relieving force of all. Again starving, sick and exhausted, they made a last assault, with the energy and unity of despair, spurred on by visions and the belief that they had discovered the holy lance. Their Turkish opponents broke and fled, leaving the crusaders, freed from the unifying force of fear, to quarrel amongst themselves over the government of the new principality. It took a further six months and a threat of mutiny among their followers before they settled their disputes and continued on their march.

The principality, which survived for 170 years, also earned a reputation for luxury. It was the richest of all the crusader states, but when it fell to the Mameluke Sultans of Egypt, the devastation was absolute: the entire population was massacred or enslaved, the gold and silver ornaments were made into heaps in the streets, and the conquering army was rewarded with coins measured by the bowlful. It never recovered. The eastern trade moved to Aleppo, and Mongols, Ottomans and earthquakes did the rest.

As, in spite of nine months of intermittent trying, I still had no visa for Syria, I had to stop and ring both London and Damascus to contract friends who were helping to extract one from the unwilling Syrian authorities. We had no diplomatic relations; British visitors were therefore unwelcome, and someone who was trying to cross on his way to enemy-occupied Jerusalem, by horse, must be both mad and of evil intent. Suspicion has become the natural state of mind of the Syrian government, towards its own people and the rest of the world alike. My saving grace was, perhaps, that I *was* mad. In the Arab world people are both kind to and very tolerant of those so afflicted by God. It took, nevertheless, four days and nearly £100 in telephone calls, stuffing endless coins into non- or rarely functioning telephone boxes, as calls from the hotel were at least twice as expensive.

But these days in Antakya did not hang heavily on my hands; it is a pleasant town to be in. There is a fine collection of mosaics in the museum, the remains of the sixth-century walls clamber over Mount Silpius behind for a distance of nineteen miles, and the views from the top and from the ruins of the citadel just a little lower to the north are glorious. I also had to see the Ministry of Agriculture about a veterinary certificate for the horses, buy farriers' tools so I could shoe a horse in emergencies myself and a new set of tools for running repairs to the cart.

The hotel television remained on all day, showing the Olympics, with renewed excitement and pride at each replay of the Turkish gold medallist's feat, and as I sat watching, I was joined by a couple of Dutch tourists, a retired ship's officer and his wife.

We were talking in the foyer when Huseyin arrived back from Iskenderun, where he had returned to pay for the new pony, and together, he and I invited them for a drive around the town in the cart. As we trotted round,

Huseyin was on his best party manners and at his most amusing, insisting on an occasional pause to buy bottles of beer for all the party. In the excitement of it all, the couple insisted on giving us supper in the evening and we trooped off to a good restaurant, where Huseyin ordered the local delicacies and a more than adequate supply of raki. He continued to entertain with party tricks of fruit carved into the shapes of heads and balanced on the rapidly emptying bottles, until we finally made our way back to the hotel with our entertainer trailing a few yards behind us, softly crooning soulful Turkish songs. When we reached the hotel, he announced, with a gasp of anguish, that he had lost his wallet and ran back to the restaurant in pursuit of it.

The morning brought no news of the wallet and a very deflated Huseyin, who was obviously fit for nothing very much for the next twenty-four hours, so I saddled Murat and rode him nervously around the town, in very heavy traffic, to exercise us both, before continuing to pursue my Syrian visa on the telephone. It was an uncomfortable business, pushing an anxious horse, unridden for some months, through the crowded back streets, in and out of cars, vans and market stalls. Murat shied and backed into a parked car at one point, but no damage was done and the crowd were sympathetic and helpful.

When, eventually, I got through to Damascus, Dr Darwish, a Syrian friend of friends who had agreed to sponsor my visit, told me that the visa had, at last, been granted but I had to collect it from the customs post on the road to Aleppo and not on the coast road as I had planned. The admirable doctor had been nagging at the authorities for days but told me that, as he was leaving for Vienna in three days' time, we would not be able to meet, but if I needed any further help I should contact his nurse, Fadwa, at Nebk and as I would be passing there anyway, should call in on her family.

The summer heat had returned with a last expiring gasp, so we delayed leaving until the late afternoon of the following day. The cobbles in the *han* were deeply rutted and uneven and as the horses started to take up the strain of the cart, Murat shied again in panic and nearly overturned it, twisting the rubber rim of one wheel out of its track in the process. Levering and hammering the rim back into place delayed us a further hour, but the road, once we were on it, proved to be much easier and more level than the one I had reconnoitred. We trotted steadily across bare, dull countryside until, an hour or two after dusk, we halted by another petrol station, throwing our sleeping bags on the ground in the adjoining field. Over the inevitable glasses of tea with the pump attendants, I sat silent, listening to Huseyin's ever-expanding stories of my importance and social significance. By the time we clambered into our sleeping bags, I had become a personal friend of Kenan Evren, the President of Turkey, with neo-royal connections.

The shallow dip in the ground beside the petrol station, where we had parked the cart in the dark, gave us an even more difficult start than the rutted *han*. Murat instantly started playing up and when Huseyin plied the whip, he backed and turned sharply, overturning the cart and breaking the pole. Huseyin and I extracted ourselves, undamaged, from the tumbled heap, amid a torrent of incomprehensible oaths that, at another time, I would have been glad to add to my own Turkish vocabulary. However, now was not the time; Huseyin had again lost face, we had the cart to set up, shafts to replace and two overexcited horses, to say nothing of an overexcited groom, to pacify. We dragged the cart from the little dell onto the road, removed the broken pole and replaced it with the shafts for a single horse, which we had kept for emergencies in the back of the cart, and set off for the last town before the frontier, with Murat alone pulling, the penalty for his bad behaviour.

At the town, Reyhanlı, a rather oppressive crowd gathered, fingering everything and clambering all over the cart, which I guarded while Huseyin went in search of a carpenter. As I struggled to prevent twenty or thirty teenagers dismantling everything they touched or upsetting the horses more than they were already, a local journalist appeared and insisted on taking photographs and asking endless questions about the trip, with the irritating persistence of a wasp round a jam jar.

In due course, Huseyin arrived with a new pole which, as he had not taken the broken pole with him as a measure, did not fit and so I told him to go back and get the job done properly. However, the carpenter had disappeared and a further hour was spent in finding a substitute, by which time, tempers all round were becoming a little frayed and Huseyin's self-confidence was dissolving like sugar in hot Turkish tea. At last the task was finished and we re-harnessed the horses, but they had had so disturbing a day that they both played up badly, reducing Huseyin almost to a jelly, so when we reached the main road again, only five kilometres from the frontier post, he said he was returning home.

'You agreed,' I said, 'to come with me to the frontier, and if you want the balance of your pay, you are coming to the frontier post.'

'But I will be very late,' he pleaded.

'I don't mind how late you are. Your driving has got the horses into this state, so you can help me sort them out or you get nothing.'

With a groan of misery and an expression like a sick spaniel, he climbed back up into the cart and continued with me for the last hour, totally subdued, and fled, with a very hurried farewell, the instant we reached the frontier. Poor Huseyin – the disasters of the last day or so were more than he could take.

I sailed through the immigration formalities and was just passing the last barrier between Turkey and the seven kilometres of no man's land that divides it from Syria, when I was stopped by a guard and turned back. I had not got customs clearance. I drove back the half-mile to the customs officers' office and asked what was the problem.

'It is forbidden to take any livestock out of Turkey,' came the reply. The customs officer's tone was not aggressive or unpleasant in any way; he just stated the regulations.

'Look, at the beginning of this journey, I consulted the Turkish Jockey Club about it and no objections were raised. Last week I asked about the necessary documentation at the customs post on the Latakia road and was told there was no problem about taking the horses across. Now, after having driven 1,200 kilometres, you tell me I can't take the horses out. What will the world say when it reaches the press? Does the Turkish government wish to be known as a bureaucratic bungler that has stopped a charitable fundraising project whose main beneficiaries are fellow Muslims in the occupied West Bank?' Frustration and anger gave my Turkish unusual lucidity.

'Can't you sell the horses here and buy more on the other side of the frontier?'

'And will you indemnify me for the inevitable loss that that will entail and help me pull the cart, by hand, across the intervening seven kilometres?'

'Oh,' was the only comment that the potentially helpful, but helpless young man could make. 'Could you wait and I will consult my colleagues?'

He returned a few minutes later. 'Will you be bringing the horses back to Turkey?'

'No, I will sell them at the end of the journey, in Jerusalem or Jordan.'

'Well, as long as you do not bring them back and say that they came from Turkey, we will close our eyes and not keep any record of it. But you must promise that, or I will be in trouble personally. I wish you every success for the rest of the trip.'

A last ritual glass of Turkish tea was consumed with the kindly and courageous official and his colleague before I drove again into no man's land to waves and happy smiles. Even the horses responded and trotted off gaily, without any of the tantrums that had marred the earlier part of the day. Crossing Turkey had taken me nearly six months; it took the First Crusade almost two years.

VI

Syrian Desert and Crusader Castles

When I found myself in the long queue of juggernaut lorries at the Syrian frontier post, the absurdity of the whole enterprise struck me even more forcibly than usual: there, in the middle of some fifty lorries, sat Quixote in a cart. As the lorries edged forward, they left a gap for me to pass through and waved me up to the front. I parked the cart beside the immigration office, tethered the horses to a convenient steel post and went in search of water. I then wandered into the office to enquire about the procedure for clearing the cart through the customs. Amused officials told me that I would need clearance from the public health officer, who had already gone home for the night, so I would have to wait until the morning.

I knew that my Arabic, which had once been fluent, was now rusty, but I was unprepared for the effect on it of six months speaking only Turkish; although I could understand what was said to me, I was quite incapable of a coherent reply. Every time I opened my mouth, out fell a jumble of bad Turkish. Lorry drivers from half a dozen countries gathered around the cart and asked about my journey; one came from the West Bank and knew the St John Eye Hospital, towards which I was heading. When I had fed and watered the horses, rugs and kettles were taken from lockers in the sides of the juggernauts and I was invited to join the drivers for tea and a meal. We talked, or tried to, over the hum of the chiller-unit engines of a dozen refrigerated lorries, until I climbed into my sleeping bag in the back of the cramped cart. It was not too uncomfortable except for the small creepy-crawlies that emerged from the bags of straw and barley to join me in bed.

The frontier post came to life at half-past eight and I began the process of customs clearance and sorting out my visa. As I had the number of the telex reference for the visa, this did not present a great problem, but its validity was to be for fourteen days only.

'But I cannot guarantee that I can drive the four hundred kilometres from here to Jordan in fourteen days; it entirely depends on the fitness of the horses.'

'Unfortunately, we are only allowed to issue visas for a fortnight from here. You must reapply when you get to Damascus, but if they are willing to issue the visa in the first place, they are unlikely to object to an extension. I am sorry we cannot be more helpful, but it is beyond our powers,' explained the immigration chief, when he had stopped laughing.

The public health officer was easier: he looked at and approved my veterinary certificate and gave a quick glance at the horses and cart.

'You have come all the way from Istanbul in that?' he said, pointing, wide-eyed, at the cart.

'More or less,' I replied.

'*Wallahi*, that is something, a marvel. The horses look fit, there is no problem.'

The last remaining hurdle was clearing the customs. The head of customs stared at me with a broad grin.

'It is very difficult,' he said. 'There are no rules about bringing horses and carts into Syria. I have had to ring Damascus and ask the department there, but they do not know either. I think that if I charge you $25 and give you an official receipt with lots of government stamps, that will keep everybody happy. OK?'

'OK.' I was led off by his assistant to change the appropriate money at the bank – so much for the customs, another bit for the visa, other small sums for this and that. The official receipts, which I was told I must not lose, piled up in the cart.

'Now you are free to go. Welcome to Syria, and good luck.'

I harnessed the horses and hoped anxiously that they would not play up and blacken my face before the crowd, a very Arab reaction; my *sharaf*, my honour, suddenly became important to me in this absurd situation. They behaved immaculately and trotted away at a cracking pace. The formalities had taken the entire morning and a mile from the frontier, a hundred lorries were drawn up awaiting the afternoon convoy. As I passed the drivers all got out, clapping and cheering – it was very heartening.

Syria was not new to me. In the course of the previous ten years I had visited it on two or three occasions and had explored as many crusader castles as I could reach. The castles had for some years been almost an obsession of mine, and in the spring, Jebel Ansariyah, the mountain range where most of them are to be found, is one of the most spectacularly beautiful places I know, densely carpeted with wildflowers that English gardeners sweat blood to reproduce at home. Whenever I had been there, internal politics had riven the country and produced bloodshed that, at times, reached horrific levels, but I had met with nothing but kindness and courtesy. I am very fond of Syria.

I reached the first small town, in a thunderstorm, in time for a late lunch and left the horses, looking wet and unhappy, outside the restaurant door while I ate and then drove on, with the name of a man at Idlib who kept a *han*. The rain stopped and as I travelled, passers-by hailed me and stopped me for a talk or with invitations to stay, but I pressed on for Idlib. The wet road was slippery and Murat fell and slid on his knees for twenty yards before I could get the other pony to stop. He had skinned his knees and I had to unharness him to get him back on his feet, but the damage was slight and required no more than a heavy dab of iodine.

I reached Idlib in the dark and asked for the owner of the *han*. It proved not to be a *han* in the traditional sense at all; the keeper was, by trade, a blacksmith and occasionally put up horses in his blacksmith's shop in the middle of the town. It was an ordinary shop unit with steel roller shutters, but it was dry and warm and I lashed down the canopy of the cart as tightly as I could before leaving it in the street to seek a hotel. A child led me to the first hotel, but there was no room; the second proved to be the dirtiest and the most grasping that I ever came across. It did not even have any running water. The fat and slovenly owner was ambivalent, undecided whether the gain of letting one more bed outweighed the risk of involvement with the police through putting up a foreigner. He even took me to the police station to ensure that all my papers were in order, and was promptly told by them to stop creating such a fuss and give me the bed. It was the first time I had met, in Syria, this new terror of doing anything slightly unusual that might involve being noticed by the police. I was to meet it again. Nevertheless, I was so tired that sleep came easily.

As the stable was locked and the blacksmith away, I could not leave until the middle of the afternoon, when his son came out of school. When at last the boy returned, a crowd of children and the town loafers pressed so closely around the stable door that I had difficulty in getting the horses out and harnessed. The crowd were as persistent as Middle Eastern flies and as irritating, which contrasted with the courtesy and helpfulness of the shopkeepers, from whom I had made a number of small purchases in the course of the morning. But the horses behaved and I drove out onto the dull desert road towards Hama until near dusk.

With my very short permitted spell in Syria, my route was strictly circumscribed. I had no time to deviate from the main north-south road and therefore was unable to return to the places that I had so enjoyed on earlier journeys. Thus, I could not divert to Aleppo, which was off any crusader route, but it is not far from Idlib and I had visited it on my last journey. I would have loved to have spent more time there; it is a town so full of visual surprises and has the best and least tourist-corrupted suq in the whole of the Arab world. As one walks down an unassuming side street, one is brought up short by a finely carved seventeenth- or eighteenth-century stone doorway or window, or by a glimpse through that doorway into a lovely courtyard beyond. I had once based myself at the Baron's Hotel there, in between excursions into the mountains in pursuit of castles.

The hotel itself was an experience; the dusty lounge had the usual cases of items for sale to guests that forget, somehow, to get sold, but the contents of these cases were different. In one corner stood a book and in the opposite corner a bill, dated June 1914, made out to Monsieur Lawrence. The book was open at a letter, headed *Baron's Hotel, Aleppo. Dear Mother...* It was a letter from T. E. Lawrence while travelling around Syria, doing his thesis on crusader castles. The hotel had not changed greatly from that time and the same family still ran it, although for years they had been tenants rather than freeholders, but there was great excitement when I was there; they hoped to win a thirty-five-year-old bankruptcy case which would recover the freehold for them. I have never heard if they did.

I stayed there five days, on and off, going out to dinner elsewhere in the town each night with other guests; once with two Lebanese tearaways, twice with an Egyptian businessman from Rome, and on the last couple of nights with one of the Princes of Lichtenstein, as catholic a selection as you could find anywhere.

Each night, on our return, I would sit and talk to the

son of the house, a keen photographer like myself, on the broad balcony overlooking the street until the early hours.

'Why don't you forget about your castles for a day and go up to the Basilica of St Simeon? It is much finer than any of your castles. It is unique, a masterpiece.'

'I can't, there are too many castles and I have too little time.'

He kept pressing me about St Simeon until, on my last morning, I asked where I could catch a bus to Latakia.

'There isn't one until five o'clock this evening, and there is a lady downstairs who wants to go to St Simeon. You can share a taxi and so it will be cheap.'

The lady downstairs proved to be a perennial student in her early thirties, who resembled, more than anything else, a half-cooked steam pudding. Her conversation was as heavy as her appearance; though I tried, for the hour in the taxi, to instil some enthusiasm for the beauties of Syria, I failed and gave up. But the basilica was all that had been promised; it was breathtaking. After half an hour, I found the steam pudding slumped on a stone, looking even less cooked than ever; she had a stomach upset. I found the guardian of the site and explained the lady's problem – had he, by any chance, something for an upset stomach? But somehow my Arabic failed; where I learned it, in South Yemen, *humma* was a fever and *hulfa* diarrhoea. In northern Syria, the local jargon was obviously different. With great concern and gentleness, the guardian sat her down on a chair and poured a bucket of cold water over her head, convinced she had heatstroke.

Unwillingly, I bundled the even more distressed lady

back into the taxi for Aleppo and listened to her tirades about the lack of sympathy and beastliness of the locals. My explanations of their good, if misdirected, intent ran off her as coldly as the bucket of water had done earlier. But I had taken, accidentally, the best photograph I have ever taken; enlarged to four feet square and printed in sepia, it still hangs on my dining-room wall. But so much for Aleppo; this time I had to miss it.

When I stopped at a village that evening, I was welcomed by a family who led the horses to a walled enclosure, fed me a supper of cracked wheat pilaf and suggested that I slept on the raised forecourt where we had supped. There is great contentment, after a successful day, in lying on the ground staring at the stars. There is a strange little constellation, like a cornucopia, three cigarette lengths from the bottom of Cassiopeia, that one can only see when one is not really looking at it; stare directly at it and it vanishes.

The father of the family admired Murat and wanted him to serve his mare, but as Murat was already up to his tricks that morning, I feared the mare would make him even more difficult to control and so made excuses about my need to hurry and left. I stopped briefly for a glass of tea in Marat an Noman, a drab industrial town, and pulled up again later at a restaurant beside the ruins of an old *han*. After a good meal and a glass of arak, I checked my map and found that I had already covered twenty-five miles and felt that that was sufficient for the day. As I unpacked the cart, I discovered that my saddlebags had been rifled in Marat an Noman and my remaining camera had been stolen.

With my hands always full of horse, I had taken remarkably few photographs; it takes time and patience to take good photographs and my time and patience had been devoted entirely to horses. I was always nervous that, had I concentrated more on photography, I would have been left standing, camera in hand, in the middle of Anatolia or somewhere, while the horses disappeared over the horizon or the cart turned over in a ditch.

I cut a ridiculous enough figure as it was without having to trail forlornly across the countryside asking strangers, 'Please sir, have you seen my horse and cart? I've lost it.' Thus my camera had spent most of its time buried in the bottom of a saddlebag, and the best photographs I had taken were still in it. I was sad rather than angry, for the camera was a good one and an old friend that had travelled with me for years. But there was, perhaps, a touch of poetic historic justice: the crusaders, on raids from Antioch, had been accused of cannibalism at Marat an Noman, so this was a tiny, inadvertent, nine-hundred-year-old bit of getting one's own back.

The restaurateur was shocked and sympathetic; local honour was impugned. As I intended to stay for the rest of the day, he offered me either space in a guest room at the back of the restaurant for the night or, if I preferred, the flat roof to sleep on. I chose the roof, for the pleasure of watching the stars, and lazed away the rest of the day looking at the vaulted ruins of the old *han* and talking to the amiable patron and the passers-by who dropped in for tea, coffee or a meal.

The ruins were not distinguished or datable from any architectural feature, but they were certainly a couple of centuries old; the site, perhaps, much older, for it lies on one of the oldest trade routes in the world, the Incense Route, that began on the southern coast of Arabia and followed the edge of the desert along the foot of the mountains of the Yemen, through Mecca and Medina to Petra and the Hellenic cities of Syria and Asia Minor. It was this trade route that supported the wealth of the Queen of Sheba, whose ancient kingdom straddled the borders of North and South Yemen and among whose runs I had lived, some twenty-five years before.

In the night, another convoy of juggernauts rumbled past, bound for Jordan, Iraq, Saudi Arabia and the Gulf, the linear descendants of those centuries of traders with their horses, donkeys and camels, but very few now stop at the *han* of Khan Shaykhun; today's journeys are measured in hundreds rather than tens of miles.

A cooling breeze eased the morning's travel, but between the *han* and Hama, there was nowhere to stop, not even a cafe, and the countryside was drab. A couple of young men on motorbikes stopped me for a gossip and one of them ran down a bank beside the road into a vineyard and returned with a present of a couple of bunches of fine white grapes, the last of the season. After four or five hours, I reached the outskirts of Hama and asked if there was another *han*. Initially, the answers from bystanders in the street were non-committal.

'I don't know.'

'There isn't one any more.'

Several years earlier, Hama had been the centre of an attempted coup d'état, for which the Hamawis had paid a terrible price. The army had besieged the town and bombarded it for days, laying waste much of the centre and reputedly killing ten thousand people. In the rebuilding, *hans* were not replaced; their survival had already been an anachronism. A taxi driver joined the group I was asking.

'Yes, there is still one,' he said. 'Follow me.' He set off through the crowded streets and I followed at a full canter, perilously weaving in and out of traffic, stalls and pedestrians until we stopped in front of a pair of old wooden gates in a wall. The *han* keeper was out, but his assistant told me to bring the horses into the small open courtyard. The keeper returned a few minutes later, a small, plump man with an expression that suggested a combination of indigestion and problems with blocked drains.

'No room,' he said abruptly, without an apology or a smile.

'Oh, my brother, you can see my horses are exhausted. Let me leave them for an hour or two and I will then take them away.'

He did not deign to answer, just turned away and talked to someone else. The Hamawis have always had a reputation for xenophobia. I left the horses and crossed the road to a more welcoming kebab stall for lunch. When I returned, I found that a crowd had gathered around the cart which I'd parked in the street in front of the rickety *han* doors, full of friendly curiosity.

'Where are you from?'

'How much did you pay for the horses?'

'Where did you get the cart?' All the usual questions rolled out and I gossiped for a while before beginning to harness the horses. At that point, the *han* keeper rushed out with his hand out and a new expression of unabashed greed on his face.

'Twenty-five pounds,' he snapped. Now, twenty-five Syrian pounds is about 75p – hardly a great imposition – but as payment for nothing more than ill manners and surliness, I found it excessive. As I dropped the notes into his fat and grasping hand, I turned to the crowd.

'Where is the honour of the Arabs? I thought the Israelis had only reached Quneitra, but it appears that some of them got as far as Hama!'

A titter of amusement broke out amongst the crowd, and the keeper fled back into the shadowy caverns of his *han*, pursued by cries of 'Shame, shame' from the amused onlookers. At the same moment, I realised that my Arabic had now returned.

The road from Hama rises quickly and steeply out of the Orontes Valley and after a couple of hours I turned into a village to find out where I could park both cart and horses for the night. A young man with a blond-bearded face, like a picture of Christ in an illustrated children's Bible, led me to his house. Food appeared for both me and the horses, followed by a gathering of neighbours and, as we lounged on cushions on the forecourt, conversations developed on politics, history, religious argument, all equally free and without rancour.

'You British were the founders of Israel, with the Sykes-Picot agreement,' complained the Syrians.

'Yes, perhaps, but who gave you your independence from the French?'

'I don't understand how you Christians worship the Trinity.'

'Nor do I,' I replied.

Conversations in Syria range much more widely round the world than in Turkish villages, possibly because of my greater command of the language, but only in part. The Syrians have a history with which they can identify, that runs back at least to the beginning of Islam in the seventh century, whereas the Turks do not often look further back than Atatürk, a penalty of the new Turkish alphabet which, for all its virtues, has cut off the past from everyone but the scholar. I have even heard educated Turks complaining that in the new, Westernised Turkish, which has been ousting Arabic and Persian words for years, they find it difficult to express themselves.

An aggressive young army officer in the party complained about the Syrian diplomats being expelled from London.

'But what would you do if a foreign ambassador was found by a Syrian court to have supplied terrorists with bombs in Damascus, which were foisted on an innocent woman?'

The rest of the party agreed and the officer changed the subject quickly. Eventually the party broke up and I was lent a pair of pyjamas so that my host's wife could wash my clothes for me and have them dry by the morning.

I left the horses resting for a day and returned by bus to Hama to look at the town and do a little shopping. The Orontes, in Antioch, runs through the town in a blank gash banked by concrete, but in Hama it is much more sinuous. In Turkey it has become a no-nonsense male, but here it is sensuously female, even where it turns the huge, protesting waterwheels that have watered the town and the surrounding land for centuries.

I went to the central post office and rang the admirable Dr Darwish in Damascus; he had arranged an extension to my visa that I could collect from the chief of police in Damascus when I got there. Then I tried to buy stamps for letters back to England. The central post office had run out but, they said, if I tried the newsvendors' stalls around the town, I might find some there. Perambulating round the town from newsvendor to newsvendor, I met the restaurateur of Khan Shaykhun who greeted me like a long-lost friend and joined me in my stamp search; in the end we found a man with a grubby envelope full of them, tucked in a drawer beneath his counter. For an hour we walked together around the town; while he did his marketing for the restaurant, I just looked at stalls, shops and people. I bought a pair of sandals, size 45. I take 47s, but in Syria they do not make anything larger than 45s, so they had to do. I enjoyed my potterings; there are still pretty doors in Hama, and stonework, like Cairo's, in alternating bands of ochre and white or black and white. It has a pleasing air of dereliction and seduction and pretty Bedawi girls, in their tall, colourful headdresses, walk through the streets with free, swinging movements like young queens. I returned to the village towards dusk with a load of biscuits and chocolates for my host's children. I had discussed what to buy as a small present for the children at length, over a cup of coffee, with my friend the restaurateur.

From Hama to Homs is the standard caravan journey

of a day, twenty-five miles; it is dull travelling, or would have been if I had not had problems, which changed it from dull to trying. The Orontes Valley cuts under the road in a ravine, halfway between two towns. At this point, a bridge spans the river on one of the fastest stretches of dual carriageway in the whole of Syria; fast, that is, for cars, but not for Murat. He looked at the wide metal expansion joint in the middle of the bridge, skewed the cart sideways and again pulled the tyre out of its rim. Still in the middle of the bridge, I took off the wheel and hammered back the tyre as cars rushed past, rocking the unstable cart with their wind. I replaced the wheel and tried again and again to get Murat across the offending joint, eventually succeeding only when I blindfolded him and led him over. It took a perilous and unnerving hour to cross the bridge.

I followed the bypass around Homs – I had been there before and my memories were mixed. I had come down from Jebel Ansariyah, tired, dirty and hungry, seven years before, to find a hotel where I could wash both myself and my clothes. The hotel had no restaurant and the staff there suggested that I went to any of those in the adjoining street. I found one and was drinking a glass of beer while waiting for my kebab, when two men had a quarrel just in front of me and one shot the other dead. Years later, it became a rather undisciplined poem.

The Syrian Restaurant

The brightness of the place attracted me,
Strong shapes of clean white tables, crisply lit;

The clean geometry, the space, the calm,
Contrasted with the crowded night outside.
The diners, few as yet, were drinking beer
Or arak, opalesque, amid the plates
Of bread and olives, hummus and kebabs;
A fleet of dishes moored about each glass.
Then came two men, whose low but bitter words,
In muted argument about a car,
Grew louder, fiercer, till the waiters moved
To soothe and separate, restore the calm,
But then it burst.
A pistol drawn
Hurled frightened waiters down behind the bar,
A clutch, a bottle seized and then the shot:
A young man, like an ill-tied parcel laid
In sticky streams of blood and lemonade.
The shock. The silence. Diners disappeared
Before the uneasy street stampeded in
And stared.
There seemed a moment when, perhaps, I could
Have intervened, have grasped the killer's arm;
I hesitated, wondered if I should,
If it might cause an even greater harm.
The moment passed: shamed by my impotence,
I left too large a tip and slipped away,
A coward's penitence.
The brightness of it had attracted me
Strong shapes of clean white tables, crisply lit;
The clean geometry, the space, the calm,
Contrasted with the crowded night outside.

So I did not regret missing Homs; I had seen enough of it, and from the bypass I could just make out a wen on the crest of the hills to the west, the incomparable Krak des Chevaliers, the greatest castle that the crusaders ever built and the masterpiece of the Knights Hospitaller, the master castle-builders of the age.

I have forgotten exactly when I first visited it; perhaps nine or ten years before, when I was driven up there with my travelling companion, Hilary Costa Sanseverino, by an anxious American diplomat with whom Hilary had been staying in Damascus. The internal strife of Syrian politics had reached one of its many peaks at that time as the Muslim Brotherhood, a clandestine opposition group, was murdering government officials at the rate of one a day, to which the government was responding with a violence on an even greater scale that culminated in the massacre at Hama.

It was wet and cold, with a mist swirling around the towers and blanking off all but the closest views, but even in the steady drizzle, we stared at a sight of immense dramatic power. Here, in Syria, stood a French Gothic castle which, in elegance, could match any early cathedral and yet was the most advanced and sophisticated piece of military engineering of its time.

The Crusaders learned to build castles from bitter necessity. The first arrivals had, at home, built only the traditional Norman keeps, which they repeated at first in Syria; they also took over a number of Byzantine fortresses as they conquered the new territory, but these were equally unsuited to their needs. The fortresses were designed to house garrisons and not to withstand long sieges; with large standing armies, Byzantine military strategy was based on these armies taking the field, but their chronic lack of manpower compelled the crusaders to devise walls that would act in lieu of men. The sophistication of European medieval military architecture developed from this experience in the Holy Land.

Krak is the supreme example; it has all the military devices of the age: double concentric circles of walls, bent entrances where the unwary attacker could be trapped and slaughtered by well-sheltered men from above, and round towers projecting beyond the curtain walls for improved fields of fire and to enfilade the flanks of the besiegers. Yet the airy room in the master's tower is decorated with stone bosses carved into flowers, and the knights' loggia has the grace and delicacy of a cloistered abbey. No wonder it contains the carved Latin reminder *Have plenty, have wisdom and beauty, but beware of pride which defiles all it touches*. How could the masters of such a place not be proud? Even when at last it fell, in 1271, it did not fall by assault, but by a *ruse de guerre*, as Baibars, the Mameluke Sultan of Egypt, is alleged to have forged a letter from the Grand Master commanding the surviving knights to surrender after he had breached the outer walls, but was still faced with the massive and impenetrable central keep.

That tour with Hilary, an intrepid and imperturbable traveller, produced other equally dramatic moments; we reached the other great Hospitaller castle in Syria, Marqab, on the coast near Baniyas, late one afternoon. It proved to be closed that day and so I suggested that we could try again the following morning.

'I have not climbed all the way up this damned hill for nothing. Where is your crusading spirit, you lily-livered Hospitaller?' So we found a stretch of wall that had crumbled to a level of ten feet and, putting an arm under that elegant backside, I pushed and we were in. The sole occupant was a braying donkey, although the adjoining ridge was better defended; it was an army camp bristling with Russian SAM missiles.

The reprimand was appropriate from the wife of a man whose ancestor had been the *bailli*, or viceroy, of the dying Kingdom of Jerusalem in the year that Krak had fallen, but I had my revenge that evening. As we sat in my room in the hotel at Baniyas, downing a glass of our last bottle of whisky, a bomb was thrown from a passing lorry, not at the hotel, but at the adjoining government shop. It exploded with a crash and a splintering of glass, but did little damage.

Hillary had been carefully instructed by her American diplomat friend: 'If anything happens, hit the floor.' She obediently hit the floor and spilled her glass of whisky. I picked her up off the grubby strip of carpet and refilled the glass. A few minutes later, the same lorry rumbled past again and threw a second bomb; it was as ineffective as the first except that it had Hilary again spreadeagled on the carpet with another empty glass. It was my turn to remonstrate.

'If you must keep prostrating yourself, put your glass down first – the Hospitaller whisky supply is very low and that spirit is irreplaceable.'

She was the most uncomplaining fellow traveller one could hope to find. It would have been easier to laugh in the bad moments with the horses, had she been there.

Another of these bad moments occurred that evening, if a minor one. I turned off onto a track leading to a village, but it was so deeply rutted and uneven that Murat panicked again and before I could calm him, the tyre was off once more. It was an hour of hammering and levering before it was mended and the cart free from the ruts, by which time it was dark. However, the villagers, as always, were helpful and hospitable, even if my host for the night was about the stupidest and clumsiest that I met on all the journey.

Scenically, the road from Homs to Damascus is universally dull, an endless succession of low, stony hills devoid of vegetation or any feature except an occasional cluster of houses, those nearest to the road adorned with political graffiti extolling the virtues of the ruling party, the Ba'ath or Renaissance Party, or the president himself. In odd spots, in the middle of nothing at all, presidential megalomania rose to its height with a statue of the unloved president with arms outspread, addressing the empty waste. To the west, the Anti-Lebanon Mountains filled the horizon and provided Syria with the few luxuries it could afford, for the obscure mountain tracks harbour a prosperous smuggling trade conducted, largely, on mules.

On the first evening, I stopped in a village and, refusing offers of accommodation, camped on a stretch of wasteland and slept in the cart. Before settling down, I went to the village shop for a wick for my hurricane lamp, which the gentle, patriarchal owner fitted for me before giving me my first cup of bitter Arab coffee of the journey. Devised by the Bedu over the centuries, its bitterness is a means of appearing to quench the thirst in places where water is often as much a luxury as a necessity, and the service of it has evolved into the ritual of hospitality. Made with cardamom roasted and ground with coffee beans, it is an acquired taste, but I love it. In the Yemen, the cardamom pods are usually replaced by ginger, an aesthetically less satisfying combination, but with the same aim and effect. My refusal of accommodation could not prevent the crowd that gathered round the cart from offering something. At dusk a small boy brought me some supper of bread, apples and tomatoes, which I ate with gusto and gratitude.

The following afternoon I reached Nebk, the town where Dr Darwish's nurse, Fadwa Shaqqa, lived. I drove the cart to the door of her brother's business, a garage, and was instantly overwhelmed by kindnesses. Fadwa was still in Damascus, but her brothers and sisters-in-law took me in hand, washing and repairing my clothes, arranging stabling with a cousin, and as I sat, feeling rather sorry for myself with a heavy cold descending, a succession of other relatives flowed in and out of the house. I was not the only guest for supper that night; two Saudis had had car trouble and while the eldest brother brought them back to the house to join the party, the younger finished the repairs to enable them to continue their journey. The lateness of the hour in no way affected the obligation to help distressed travellers.

I left the horses for a day in the hands of the Shaqqa

cousin and shared a service taxi into Damascus, for I needed to speak to the last remaining British diplomat and to change some money at a bank. The taxi driver epitomised today's Syria. Helpful and friendly, he drove to Malki, the diplomatic quarter of Damascus, but did not know the exact location of the British Embassy, now masquerading under the Australian flag because of the break in relations. The area was full of young men at street corners with ominous bulges around their waistbands or under their armpits.

'I don't like to ask the way,' he explained. 'They are all *mukhabarat*, secret police, and I am afraid to get involved.' I relieved him of his anxiety by getting out and asking the way myself. The nearest secret policeman directed me, with courtesy and a smile, to the appropriate street. The last time I was in Syria, people I met spoke of the government with disgust. Now they did not dare to speak at all.

That evening, Fadwa arrived home and, horrified that I did not possess a pullover, produced one from a drawer and pressed it on me, brushing aside my protests.

'It is getting cold now, you will need it.' She was right: it was noticeably colder the following day and I was very grateful for it.

The next day's start was not auspicious. The horse-minding cousin's teenaged sons had been riding the horses and had unsettled them, so it took nearly an hour to calm them and get them underway. The Shaqqa family loaded me with food, enough maintain an army, for the last stretch to Damascus. Again, my protests were swept aside.

'You will not find anywhere to buy any until you reach the city,' said Fadwa and, of course, she was right again. Unlike Turkey, the facilities for travellers are poor in Syria; the petrol-station restaurants that sustain Turkish travel are rare, for the distances between the towns are much shorter. There proved to be nowhere to stop at all for nearly forty miles, until I found, at dusk, a house that could let me have some water, and thereafter I threw down my sleeping bag on the ground a couple of hundred yards off the main road.

An early start brought me to the outskirts of Damascus by mid morning and my first enquiry about stabling, at a garage, brought an instant invitation to put both horses and cart in the adjoining orchard. I then returned to the embassy, where a car was provided to take me to the chief of police for my visa. The police general was somewhat dour as I explained my predicament, but he was cooperative and ordered an extension of the visa for a further two weeks.

With time to kill, I went down to the suq and bought myself a Bedawi sheepskin coat, for which Syria is renowned, as my present of the jersey had proved barely adequate for the onset of autumn and both Jordan and Jerusalem can be cold in October and November. The *farwa*, as it is called, is a heavy, shapeless garment of black cloth lined with shaggy sheepskin, and is warm even in the snow.

I bought the cheapest I could find and returned in the early evening to the flat of John Davies, the charming and enthusiastic diplomat in charge of the residual British interests. He had invited me to dinner in the place of an official guest from England for whom the Syrians had refused to grant a visa. Arriving early, I could luxuriate in a bath, for although elegance or even respectability were beyond me, cleanliness at least was possible. It was now many months since I had been at a normal English dinner party and the company was bright, varied and amusing, so when I took a taxi back to the horses, my spirits were high, more so because John had slipped a bottle of whisky into my pocket as I left, a restorative for the road.

I was tempted to sample it early the next morning. I made a particularly early start to try to cross Damascus before the morning rush hour, but missed my way for lack of road signs and was soon struggling in the middle of it. Damascene buses seemed to converge on the cart from every direction; they all waited until they were a few feet away and then, with a hideous cacophony of sound, blew their horns as hard and long as they could. It was a nightmare, but the horses seemed much less concerned than I was. It might have been better if I had just closed my eyes and left it to them; they could not have got more lost and my nerves would have screamed less. Eventually we were through it and I rewarded them by stopping at a fruit stall and sharing with them yet another watermelon and some grapes. The perversity of horses: when there is nothing to worry about they shy and misbehave but, in the middle of howling chaos, they plod on unperturbed and even stop automatically at red traffic lights. The nature of horses is like the peace of God; it passeth all understanding.

By the late morning I reached one of the rare rest houses and stopped for an enormous breakfast-cum-lunch of liver and side dishes, washed down with gallons of tea; I considered that I had earned it. Talking to the rest-house keeper, I found that I had travelled twenty-five miles already, so I tethered the horses in an adjoining olive grove, stretched out beneath a tree and slept.

With the party the night before and the very early start, I had only managed three hours' sleep. An hour's nap revived me and I wandered back into the rest house. I ordered a glass of tea, took out my patience cards and started to play while the owner watched for a few minutes with the odd intervening question, for patience was new to him. Then, taking my cards, he performed a succession of card tricks with great dexterity and at high speed. I could not follow the sleight of hand at all and in minutes, the waiters and I were arguing, with gusts of laughter, about how these were done, but the owner maintained a sphinx-like expression and kept his secrets. More tea and conversation flowed. I was short of fodder for the horses and asked where I could get some.

'If you turn right by the next bridge, the track will lead you off the autostrada to the old road, where there are regular villages. On the new road there are none, so you would be better off that way.'

We talked away the rest of the afternoon and, after supper, I was offered a room to sleep in to the rear and was woken, in the morning, with a glass of tea, for all the world as if I was in a proper hotel.

I bought some fodder in the first village on the old road, a slow process as the adults seemed to be away or out in the few fields and the teenagers I asked were hesitant to act without parental approval. I drove on through a countryside of unusual barrenness, flat and featureless except for the litter of black boulders that made the land unfit for the plough even when it rained. As evening approached I drove through a village – appropriately named Sheikh Maskīn or Poor Sheikh, for this was very poor country – and pulled off the road towards an isolated farmhouse. I had driven thirty miles and the horses were tired. A young man appeared from the building, a mere stone house with a single room above, whom I asked for water and permission to tether the horses there for the night.

'*Ahlain*,' he said, a Syrian and Jordanian dialect greeting, 'of course you may. Come and have some tea.' He called to an unseen sister to put on a kettle. Once in the upper room, he suggested that I should sleep there, or come with him to his family's house in the village, a mile away to the east.

'Thank you, but I like sleeping outside – I will sleep beside the cart.' The room was small and stuffy and the open air would be much fresher.

'But you will eat with us?'

'I would be honoured.'

The young man told me that the following day he was leaving to join the army for his national service. Outside I could hear the two young sisters arguing about their domestic tasks until a male voice mingled with those of the girls. A moment later, another young man came up the stairs to join us. He sat down beside me and stared at my watch.

'How much?'

'I bought it years ago, I cannot remember.'

'How much did you pay for the horses? How much for the cart? For the saddle?' He punctuated each question with an irritating stab in the ribs with his finger.

As darkness fell, my young about-to-be-a-soldier host apologised. 'I am sorry, we have no light.'

'That's all right, I have a hurricane lamp in the cart.' I went down to collect it, followed by the two young sisters, who admired my few pots and pans. As I hardly ever used them and was approaching the end of the journey, I gave the girls most of them. Their parents would not have approved of the begging looks; had they seen them, the girls would have been scolded and shooed away for such disgraceful behaviour, but they were not and I enjoyed finding a way to return the kindnesses.

Next, there was no bread, but I had some, a parting present from the people of the rest house, so that was added to the supper. With supper over, the two girls jumped onto a single small pony and cantered, bareback, to the village and I left the two young men, still talking in the gloom of my hurricane lamp, to lay out my sleeping bag under the stars.

The rough track back to the road made Murat play up again, delaying a planned early start. The two young men walked with me for the first half-mile, putting their shoulders to the back of the cart in the deeper ruts, and then, with an exchange of good wishes, we parted. I drove on through the arid, boulder-strewn land, stopping only to buy cigarettes, to Dera'a, the last town in Syria. It was at Dera'a that T. E. Lawrence, disguised as a peasant, had in 1917 been caught and tortured by the Turks. He returned a year later, with the Arab army, to capture the town in one of the bloodiest and most significant battles of the Arab Revolt, for Dera'a was a railway centre where the lines to Mecca, Palestine and Egypt diverged. But politics and a divided Arab world have deprived it of its significance and left it a small, dusty frontier town; a halt on journeys to other places, where bureaucracy imposes its own brief delay to stamp a passport and inspect baggage.

I spent an hour in the deep wadi that runs through the southern edge of the town, to rest the horses, before struggling up the arduous slope that leads to the Jordanian frontier. The raped and battered Lawrence had escaped down this valley, then empty, but now incorporated in the growth of the town. I searched my disordered piles of baggage for the handful of receipts I had been told to preserve, two weeks before on the northern frontier. I waved them at the immigration and customs officials, who barely looked at them and bid me cheerful and friendly goodbyes.

It was a relief to cross the frontier. For all my affection for Syria and Syrians and their unfailing kindness, the politics had this time been a permanent anxiety. What would have happened if I had lost another horse and had to delay? The horror of failure through some political quirk, after a journey of seven months and over a thousand miles, always hovered in the darker corners of my mind. The frontier crossing was also a landmark: I was on the last straight, if not quite the last furlong, and I was desperately tired. Even successful and trouble-free days could not now lift me out of my weariness.

A smartly dressed, if surprised Jordanian policeman greeted me at the top of the slope that led down to the frontier post. I explained about my means of travel and the objective, adding for good measure that I had the personal approval of Queen Noor, the patron of the Friends of the Hospital, to whom I had spoken the previous year in England.

'It is, of course, forbidden to bring horses into Jordan, but in view of the aim, there can be no objection.' He waved me on with a smile and a salute.

The quarter-mile slope down to the frontier post was steep and the tarmac surface slippery. Murat slid and stumbled and was unwilling to go on, but gentle cajoling and the impetus of his characterless and still nameless but implacable companion carried him past the painted barriers. He was almost too tired to resist.

I halted the cart in the car park, where the weary horses waited patiently for the half an hour it took to clear the immigration hurdles and then trotted on towards Ramtha. A few hundred yards down the road I asked a lone youth where I could put the horses.

'Here,' he said, 'in the pilgrim town.' We were passing a high wall which proved to be the compound, known as the pilgrim town, where the government provides temporary accommodation for the busloads of pilgrims travelling on the annual journey to Mecca, but the pilgrim season was long past and the compound was empty. The boy opened the gate, led me into the large, empty compound and showed me a tap where I could water the horses.

'They will be all right here, I will guard them.'

'Thank you very much. Tell me, what is your name?'

'Muhammed.'

'Muhammed, is there a hotel here?'

'Yes, you have passed it, two hundred metres up the road.'

As I began to tend the horses, Muhammed asked, 'Can I ride the little one? I like that horse.'

'No, it is very tired and needs at least a day's rest.'

He lost interest and disappeared, while I finished the chores and made my way back to an almost-clean bed in the hotel and a shower.

In the morning, the little horse had disappeared. I walked across the road from the compound to the nearest sign of activity, a garage, whose owner proved to be a Turk from Antakya, who had settled in Ramtha some years earlier. When I told my tale, the garage owner turned his eyes towards the heavens.

'I know that boy, he is a disaster. His father, the pilgrim town guardian, is a good man, but the boy! We had better go and see the father. Jump in.' He pointed to a pickup truck.

We found the father at home a mile away and repeated the story over a cup of coffee.

'Don't worry, I will find the horse and bring it back.' The boy had even given a false name: he was Khalid, not Muhammed.

Together, we returned to the compound and moved the cart to a corner where it was less visible from outside.

'You say you want to go to Amman today. Just go and I will find my son and the horse by this evening.'

I took a service taxi into Amman, a journey of some fifty miles, to see an old friend of thirty years' standing, Mamdouh Bisharat, a landowner and farmer whom I had first met when he was a young man-about-town in London. We met very rarely these days and wrote to each other even less, but picked up where we had left off at each new meeting. I found him on his farm, at Umm al Kundum, a few miles to the south of the city. The farmhouse is a delight, an old fortified house with large vaulted rooms, dating from the middle of the nineteenth century when houses were built for defence against raiding parties from the desert tribes. It is furnished with great simplicity, sparseness and flair.

We fell on each other's necks with enthusiastic greetings. I had written a month or two before I started my journey to say I expected to arrive in June or July, but it was now mid-October and he had assumed that, for some reason or another, I had had to call the journey off. He admitted later that when this strange, drawn spectre arrived on his doorstep, he was horrified, not by my arrival, but because I looked so old. I looked nearer my mid-seventies than mid-fifties. As we drove together back to Amman, I told him that I was worried about the road from Ramtha. It passes through a tangle of mountains, dips into a deep gorge at Jerash and then climbs very steeply up again, which would be a killer for the horses.

'Why don't you go via Mafraq and Zarqa?' he said. 'It is a bit longer, but much easier and then you can avoid Amman altogether, by coming straight to Umm al Kundum. My cousin, Hani, has a riding stable here, where you can leave the horses. You can then stay here or at Jebel Jaufa for as long as you need.' Jebel Jaufa is his main family house in the centre of Amman.

Late in the afternoon, I returned to Ramtha, where my Turkish friend told me that both cart and horses had been moved to the compound guardian's house, where he could more easily keep an eye on them.

On harnessing the horses in the morning, I discovered that the boy, Khalid, had also stolen a bridle and a nosebag and disappeared yet again.

'God finish me with that boy!' cried his despairing father. 'Have you a spare bridle?'

'Yes, I have.'

'Then go on to Mafraq and I will catch you up with the stolen bridle in my pickup as soon as I can find the boy.'

The road was narrow and bad, a succession of steep, if short, desert hills filled with heavy lorries. In addition, the lorry drivers' road manners left a lot to be desired, so when I was waved down by a couple of young traffic policemen in their car in the middle of nowhere, my temper was already short.

'Why are you not driving on the verges?' they demanded. 'You will cause an accident.'

'Just look at them!' I retorted. 'If you were to maintain the verges properly, I would be delighted to drive on them, but you do not – they are a disgrace! Nothing can possibly drive on them. And as to causing an accident, I have already driven over a thousand miles without causing one, and if anything happens here, it will undoubtedly be the fault of the universally bad road manners that I have met with since arriving in Jordan!' There is nothing like anger for sharpening up the vocabulary.

The young policemen, abased by the tirade, looked at the verges, looked at each other and looked back at me, grinning.

'You are quite right. Where have you come from? Where did you learn your Arabic?'

As I began telling my story, the unfortunate guardian drew up in his pickup and returned his thieving son's loot. In a few minutes, the policemen apologised again with a smart salute and I continued on my way.

I arrived at Mafraq in a thunderstorm in the early afternoon, giving a lift and some protection from the rain to a passing pedestrian as I came into the town. He, however, proved to be no help as regards stabling, for though he shouted and waved to his friends in the street, laughing at his strange transport, he jumped off at his destination, without offering any suggestions or even a word of thanks. It was an hour before I found a suitable stretch of open ground at the edge of the town to park, and was offered accommodation by a Bedawi, now settled in the town.

A crowd of shouting children and steep, slippery streets made for another difficult start, but once out of the town the horses settled to a steady pace in spite of the endless desert hills. Pausing by the roadside, I fell into conversation with a driver who drew up beside me, out of curiosity. I asked about the possibility of somewhere to put the horses for the night at Zarqa.

'The army has a riding club there, they should be able to help you.'

So when I reached Zarqa after six hours on the road, I headed for the army headquarters and, somewhat presumptuously, asked if I could stable the horses there. The orderly officer rang through to the club secretary, who agreed, subject to my removing them the following morning. Murat had not seen such splendid facilities since the racecourse at Adana, and the little horse had probably never met anything like it in its life before. Grooms appeared with bales of hay instead of the usual chopped straw, the horses were washed for the first time for weeks and I left happily for Amman, knowing that they were in an equine equivalent of Claridge's.

Mamdouh was out for dinner when I reached there, but on his return told me that in the morning, he would lend me a man to guide me through to the farm. We collected him, a nice, cheerful young fellow, in Mamdouh's farm pickup and set off for Zarqa. At the stables were a crowd of officers and the secretary, and having had trouble starting off almost every day for the past week, I was anxious to preserve the remains of an already dubious reputation before this equestrian elite. Mamdouh's young man and I manhandled the cart to a good, level piece of hard standing before harnessing the horses, and set off at a good, steady pace without any difficulty whatsoever. Both horses were on their best party manners and I sighed with relief, for this was also going to be the last day's driving. I knew that from

Amman, it was going to be impossible to take the cart down into the Jordan Valley and up the other side, and that I would have to abandon the cart and the little horse and ride the last hundred miles.

The drive was possibly the most exacting of any on the whole journey: the traffic was heavy, the road narrow and mountainous and I was forced off it by lorries on a number of occasions. It required continuous concentration, and wore down both the horses and me. I hardly noticed the ugliness of the industrial suburbs through which we passed, for when I was not concentrating on the road, I was talking to my pleasant and enthusiastic companion, who I let drive when the road and traffic allowed. Finally, with the tired horses no longer able to achieve more than a slow walk, we dragged ourselves up to Umm al Kundum in the late afternoon, unharnessed them for the last time and led them off to the stables. There was one more frontier to cross and another hundred miles still to travel but, for the moment, I had reached the end of my tether. I was too tired to contemplate the political or the physical problems of that last short stretch.

I sat on the terrace in front of the house as a series of visitors, diplomat friends of Mamdouh, flowed past for a drink or a cup of tea but, in my exhausted state, they left no impressions, like images in a dream, people without faces, voices or form. When they had departed we drove back to Amman, stopping briefly to call in on Mamdouh's sister, Layla, a robust old friend of great kindliness and gaiety, before supper and bed.

I had still to clear the passage of Murat across to the West Bank with the Israeli authorities, and to arrange the permit to cross from Jordan with the Jordanian Ministry of the Interior. The latter was quickly arranged with a couple quick telephone calls to Queen Noor's office; the former proved to be an entirely different affair. The Israeli Embassy in London had told me months before that I would need a veterinary certificate, which I had, but that otherwise any crossing would depend only on the state of security at the time. I had already heard that Tim Severin had crossed a month or two before and thus believed that the embassy in London had meant what it said.

However, I was soon to be relieved of that illusion. The only means of contacting the Israeli authorities, without physically going to the Allenby Bridge, the sole crossing point between Jordan and the West Bank, was through the British Embassy.

The embassy was initially quite hopeful and sent a message to the Consul General in Jerusalem, but in the evening rang back with a gloomier prognostication of the likely Israeli response. At the exorbitant cost of over £30, I rang St John in London to ask if, should all else fail, the hospital could arrange a horse to meet me at the other side of the bridge.

In the meantime, I could do nothing but sit and wait: the accumulation of weariness of body and spirit bore down on me. In the midst of old and valued friends, I was lonelier and more isolated than ever. Although only a hair's breadth away from success, the achievement seemed trivial and the sum raised for the hospital insignificant, the running costs for a mere ten days. It was a piece of

Boy Scout romanticism, a mere nothing, and yet I had the arrogance to expect people to rally round and help me. My egotism disgusted me, my increasing irritability was ill-mannered and inconsiderate, and my fears of new disasters and failure haunted me more than ever.

I spent the days with Mamdouh on his other farm in the Yarmuk Valley, at the foot of the Golan Heights, dining with friends in the Jordan Valley or alone in the house on Jebel Jaufa, writing up my diary, writing letters or badgering the embassy for news. My contact there told me that they had heard from Jerusalem that the problem was bureaucratic rather than political, but there was no concrete response. Sometimes I summoned up the energy to go out to Umm al Kundum to ride Murat for an hour, as I had not ridden for months, but my tiredness and depression would not go away; all I wanted to do was to finish it all and go home.

After five days of waiting, I decided to ride down to the bridge and await further news there. But there was still the little horse to dispose of; for a month it had been a good worker, with none of Murat's tantrums, but it was so lacking in character that I could feel no real interest in or affection for it. I discussed it with Mamdouh, who had a Bedawi working for him with a knowledge of horses, so I gave him the horse as a present without the slightest pang at the parting, and the following morning, rode slowly away from Umm al Kundum on the road to the Jordan Valley.

The road was being widened and straightened and was full of construction traffic and bulldozers, which had destroyed the surface. At Naur, at the top of the escarpment I stopped to buy fodder and began the descent. It was something of a disappointment, as the views along the edge of the rift in so many places are spectacular, out across the valley, down to the Dead Sea and up to Jerusalem beyond, but the road twisted and turned in such a manner that I could rarely see anything beyond the next corner and the ravine immediately below me. A thunderstorm hovered a mile away over the upper slopes of the valley, increasing the heat and the atmospheric oppression but without the relief of rain.

By the time I reached Amasiya, halfway down the escarpment, I was already stiff and tired, with a new crop of blisters, as the rough ground and the bulldozers had meant that I had walked as much as ridden. I stopped in the village for tea and to buy some fruit, for I had foolishly refused breakfast before I started.

Gossiping with the shopkeeper, I asked if there was anywhere I could put Murat for the night, for though it was still early afternoon and I had only travelled for five or six hours, there was, unlike in Syria, no pressure on time.

'Stay with me and we can tie up the horse outside.'

I was delighted, but others appeared and an amiable argument developed regarding who was to put me up. I remained neutral until it was finally decided that the person with the prior claim was the shopkeeper's cousin, who had been in the Jordanian air force and during his service had spent a year on a radar course in Somerset.

My host had retired from the air force because of illness, but was still only in his mid-thirties, a handsome, gentle-featured man, whose once-fluent English had become rusty from lack of use. With my own diminished

Arabic vocabulary, we provided mutual support, producing the forgotten words in the other's language as the need arose. His family had come to Amasiya from the south a hundred years before, fleeing from a blood feud. The conversation revolved, all evening, around local tribal and general Arab history, the sort of conversation I had not had for over twenty years. In South Yemen, these tales of tribal origins, of blood feuds and history, sometimes running back even to pre-Islamic times, were a staple diet, part of a political officer's education and the tools of his trade, but I had been away from these things for so long that I had forgotten the pleasures of it, this strange extending of history into the present day.

It brought back memories of a blood feud I had tried to settle between two desert tribes living on the edge of the Empty Quarter, that thousand-mile expanse of dune-filled waste that divides South Yemen from Saudi Arabia and the Gulf states. It was in the late '50s or early '60s and there was one disputed killing that I could not place in time. I asked the oldest man present, a tiny, shrivelled husk of a man, when it had happened.

'I don't know,' came the reply, 'but I know that it was before my parents were married.' That would have put it, at the latest, at just before the Boer War. I managed to settle the feud by promising, in my youthful enthusiasm, to pay the blood money required to even the tribal score, a traditional sum of 733 Maria Theresa silver dollars, out of my own pocket. The Aden government bailed me out of my rash promise, but the feud broke out again a few years later. Nothing changes for long in the anarchic nature of South Yemen – anarchy is its oldest tradition.

Aden

Late sun restores the hills' contorted form
That midday bleached of colour, depth and line,
Sharp tongues of light
Now curl about the tomb whose limewashed dome,
Bright half-ellipse amid small fields of green,
Has stood for a millennium or two
To celebrate an ancient saint or sage,
A priest-king of an unremembered age.

Once he controlled a thriving incense trade
From towered cities at the desert's edge,
Where caravans of myrrh
Were halted, measured and assessed for tolls,
Till anarchy regained its old estate
And hungry nomads scoured the tumbled stones
In hope of gold the ruins might reveal,
Or some fine agate carved into a seal.

But surely he enjoyed the evening breeze
While sitting, as did I, among good friends,
Lean, dark men, sinewed like taut springs,
Quick-moving, nervous, garrulous as birds,
With bubbling laughter welling up within
At all our own absurdities.
Did he not love the evening light that fills
With ever-changing colour, those stark hills?

September, overburdened with the heat,
Makes moving of a limb an act of will.

Now patience cracks, the storms
Of blinding temper and the sand
Obliterate the landscape and the mind;
Exposure flays, the darkest recess fills
With dust and anger till pursuing rain
Restores men's reason and the land again.

But even blessings here have darker sides,
The land gives nothing, but it claims its fee;
For life-renewing floods
Renew vendettas that have run decades
And spill fresh blood to mingle with the old
In feuds of ownership of barren fields.
Neither your spells, old king, nor my vain threats
Could stop the killing that this land begets.

Old images persist. The snake-like files
Of hillmen, armed, dark-stained with indigo,
Those twisting lines of blue,
Converging from surrounding mountainsides
To hector, parley or perhaps to pledge
A doubtful loyalty to their amir:
Their chanted rhymes of tribal escapades
Crescendo with the shouts, the fusillades.

The fear, the waiting for the raids, do you
Remember that? Seeing the work of years,
A small prosperity,
Built hand on hand, dissolving in the flames?
Yet those old battles had their recompense,
Intensity, an exultation, just to be alive;

The reputation and the pride it gave.
Old king, it must be quiet in the grave.

Yet did we wish to change those wilder ways,
The pride that soared with kite and lammergeyer
In knife-edge days,
When young men sought to etch an honoured name
Upon recited epics of the tribe?
We tried on anarchy to force a form,
To press amorphous dust into a mould,
Half hoping that the pattern would not hold.

Though one apart, I also loved this land
With passion just as potent as your own,
Wept for dead friends, your heirs,
And was consoled by brothers of your tribe.
Now what remains? Some fading photographs,
Curled sepia memories of past beliefs,
Whose truths are tangled into fairy tales
And turn to myths as recollection fails.

I enjoyed that evening of retrospection; it took me away
from my weariness and worries, but nevertheless, the
weariness won soon enough and I slept early.

The road from Amasiya to the Jordan Valley was
easier and I rode most of the way. The thunderstorms
of the previous day broke into showers of rain, neither
very heavy nor prolonged, which freshened the air, and
I reached Jounieh, in the flat bed of the wadi, at midday.

The village school had just come out for lunch and
the road was full of small boys, from nine to twelve years

old, who walked beside me for a while and talked. Then suddenly there was a shower of stones. It started with a few of the larger boys to the rear of the group, and when I remonstrated, they all began throwing them. I pushed poor Murat into a canter, waved my whip like a sabre and led a one-man cavalry charge at the little beasts, making sure I dispersed them without actually getting near enough to cause any injury. They ran for cover into the centre of the village, while I cantered on to a group of shops a few hundred yards away, to vent my anger on their parents. The shopkeepers and the few customers sheepishly offered apologies, but when I suggested that one of them should speak to the headmaster of the school about this appalling lapse of Arab good manners, an expression of glazed apathy came over their faces. In a polyglot village a thousand feet below sea level, nobody does anything he can avoid doing.

I rode on, disgusted of Tunbridge Wells, to South Shuna, the last town before the Allenby Bridge. But I suppose that I can now claim, with only a slight distortion of the truth, to be the only British ex-cavalry officer living to have led a charge, however absurd; a distinction equalling in dubiety those world-champion tripe-eaters and endurance piano-playing champions.

The southern end of the Jordan Valley is a sad and depressing place. Further north it is full of prosperous, well-managed citrus farms and banana plantations, sustained by the diverted waters of the Yarmuk River. But the water supply runs out beyond South Shuna and the failure to find another solution is evidenced by abandoned orchards of stark, dead orange trees. The town itself has few attractions – a fourth-rate hotel, a few very bad restaurants and basic shops clustered around the central roundabout – but is redeemed by the people. They have come from everywhere. The hotel is run by an amiable Egyptian, some of the shopkeepers are Syrian and Pakistani, Egyptian peasants work in the market gardens, and even Bangladeshis have drifted there in search of work.

I found a farm at the edge of the town for Murat and settled into the hotel, before going out to explore the town. I drank coffee with Syrians, tea with Egyptians and had a long conversation with an old man in a greengrocer's shop about Glubb Pasha, here always known as Abu Faris and much loved. The old man had served under him forty years before. I returned to the hotel to find some new arrivals, a gaggle of Australian girls with whom I had a drink that evening and who, before leaving the following morning, left me an envelope containing the dollar equivalent of £25 for the hospital, so I killed time writing a letter to St John in London, enclosing a sterling cheque for their contribution.

For four days, I waited for news, at my wits' end to find a method of passing time. I rode Murat around the market gardens and through the citrus orchards, both the derelict and the thriving. I wrote endless letters, played endless games of patience, punctuated by glasses of tea produced by the hotelier, and took a bus to the Dead Sea rest house, twenty miles away, a quite sophisticated tourist complex with a good restaurant. The bus was driven by Jehu himself but the service taxi, on the return, hardly exceeded twenty miles an hour; the steering was so erratic the taxi wobbled all over the road with a will of its own.

Then came a message from the embassy. The Israelis would not let me over the bridge with Murat, and so I had to part with him. Of all the horses, he was the one to whom I had become most attached. For over two months, he had been my daily companion and I had led him, driven him and ridden him for nearly eight hundred miles. In spite of his occasional tantrums, he had greeted me each morning with a welcoming snicker and had become part of my life. He was handsome, amiable, without any malice and a friend.

A local made an offer for him, but I could not bear to think of him touted for rides to tourists at the entrance to the rest house, he deserved better treatment than that, so I rang Hani Bisharat, the stable-owning cousin of Mamdouh's, and offered him Murat as a present. That way he would be well housed and well looked after. Hani accepted, so I hired a small lorry and took him back, with some anguish, to Umm al Kundum.

But there was some compensation for the pain of parting: for the first time in nearly eight months, I was free from the burden and anxiety of horses. With saddle and saddlebags over my shoulder, I walked down the hill from Umm al Kundum and hitched a lift into Amman in a police car. As Mamdouh was away, I took a room in a hotel, where the arrival of a tramp with a saddle caused a sufficient stir for a reporter to appear a few hours later and write a generous article about the journey in a local daily paper.

I contacted the embassy once again and was told that there had been a bad bomb incident at Jericho, just across the Allenby Bridge. It had thrown the town into chaos and thus I would be unable to cross for a further week. The hospital would then arrange for a horse to meet me on the other side. Frustrated and desperate to finish it all, I protested and tried to get the date brought forward but to no avail: the embassy was adamant. Despairingly, I took a taxi and toured Madaba and Mount Nebo to fill in the time, but without much pleasure or satisfaction. I could think of nothing but getting to Jerusalem. From Mount Nebo I could see it, but it felt an age away. I learned that Mamdouh was at the Yarmuk Valley farm, and so rang him there.

'What are you doing in the hotel?' he asked. 'Go to Jebel Jaufa and stay there. Abu Zawdi, the driver, will bring you down here when he next comes down in a couple of days.' I packed up and crossed the city to Jebel Jaufa.

Having sat on a charitable trust for a number of years that supported two English-language medium schools in Amman, I called on the British Council representative to enquire about them and to arrange a visit, so I could report to the board at the first meeting after my return. During the years of Jordan's prosperity, we had given very little support, but with the change of financial fortunes, the schools were struggling again and the trust's small contribution of hard currency would be useful. Touring the schools in my ragged, travel-worn clothes, I felt the most unlikely inspector of schools that had ever been. At the best of times, I felt that I was an odd member of the board of trustees, for my only venture into education had been as the chairman and founding board member of the British School in Cairo, some twelve years earlier, and that came about more by accident than by design. But the schools were most hospitable to their comic-opera, raggle-taggle inspector and I was glad to be able to fill a waiting day with something useful, instead of fretting and growing more and more irritable.

Mamdouh's driver brought me down to the farm. It was a place I had known and loved for years. Mamdouh had built himself the simplest of traditional houses, years before, three square domed rooms and a separate kitchen, with natural hot water piped from a sulphur spring that also irrigated the entire farm. In the shade of date palms stands a carved Roman stone door leading to a black basalt-lined pool, fed by a gently steaming cascade. Out of the pool rises a basalt column and capital from nearby Gadara, of the Gadarene swine. Yet there is no sense of extravagance, no ostentation; an air of homely dilapidation suggests that it grew that way.

Soon after my arrival, a young architect arrived fresh from his work on the top of the hill, restoring the Turkish governor's house at Gadara, a nineteenth-century building of charm, but now sadly decayed. An engaging young man, he breathed enthusiasm; his art and the balance of the new and the traditional mattered, a fine and ever-changing judgement between knowledge and flair. Mamdouh, the architect Ammar and I sat and talked until dark.

'Will you stay the night?' Mamdouh asked him. He

stayed and the talk continued through supper and by starlight. His enthusiasm was catching and it was late by the time we had talked the world into order. Even the black shape of the Golan Heights towering behind us had vanished into the night.

Mamdouh had some business in the morning, so he left me for an hour at Gadara, where a headless marble Tyche, Goddess of Fortune, still sat in the front row of the little amphitheatre looking out at the vast backdrop of Golan, Mount Tabor, Lake Tiberias and Hattin, the graveyard of crusader ambition. The air was fresh and scented with herbs and the view incomparable. We returned to the farm where friends and family had gathered for lunch and a swim, and as the evening fell, I left for Amman; the week's waiting was up and in the morning Abu Zawdi, driver, factotum and friend, was to drive me early down to the bridge.

We reached the bridge at eight and I crossed, weighed down by four saddlebags and a saddle.

As I dumped my possessions in front of the immigration office, an Israeli soldier asked, 'Where is the horse?'

'You b******s would not let me bring it across, so there is another one awaiting me just beyond the security area.'

The soldier shrugged his shoulders and grinned. 'Don't blame me, it isn't my fault.'

The formalities only took a few minutes, and when I emerged the horse was not there. But the hospital warden's wife, the hospital superintendent and the consul were, complete with transport bearing the name of the hospital and the eight-pointed cross of St John.

'Welcome, welcome!' said Nazzar Banian, the superintendent. 'We have been waiting for you for months and getting very anxious. The horse will be here in a minute.' It was. A pickup drew up beside us with a nice little-dappled mare in the back. In half an hour, I had saddled it with my own saddle and was ready to go, with the saddlebags safely in the back of the van.

'Go straight through Jericho and keep on the main road. The road divides just before Jerusalem and we will meet you there with the van, to lead you to the hospital.'

The van led on and I was stopped a mile down the road by *The Times*' correspondent. We talked for a few minutes.

'I hope to get something in tomorrow's edition,' he said.

The little mare walked delicately, like Agag, and shied a touch at each municipal dustbin. I reached the centre of the town to find the hospital van waiting to point out the way. They indicated the direction and moved on, but I had not breakfasted so I stopped briefly for a glass of tea and a 10p bag of freshly cooked falafel, delicious balls of ground chickpeas and herbs, an old favourite of mine. The shopkeepers and bystanders were chatty and friendly; they had seen the hospital van, and the hospital is well known and admired. For a moment, I provided them with a diversion, an escape from the traumas of intifada and the reprisals, for two or three houses had been blown up a few days before in response to the bombing.

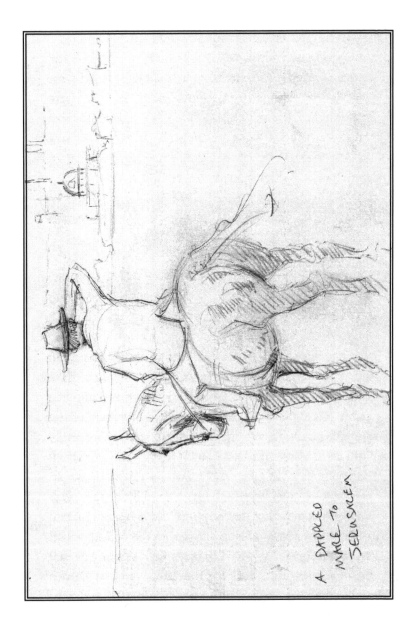

A DAPPLED
MARE TO
JERUSALEM.

I rode out of the town into one of the bleakest landscapes that I have ever met; even South Shuna was something compared with this. An Israeli patrol car, bristling with soldiers and guns, pulled up beside me and a sergeant leaned out.

'Swap transport?'

'No, I like being old-fashioned.'

He laughed, waved and drove on. An hour later, a kibbutz farmer greeted me.

'Where have you come from?'

'Istanbul.'

'Like that?'

'Yes.'

'Phew! Don't follow the road – turn off onto that track there, it is shorter and rejoins the main road an hour further on.'

'Thanks.'

I followed in the direction he was pointing, an old road, long abandoned, but still retaining a trace of tarmac here and there. It rose sharply, twisting and turning through the arid waste, and I only saw one man, a shepherd with whom I exchanged greetings but did not stop. In due course, it rejoined the main road as I had been told and soon after there was a milestone beside it, marked with a line and *SEA LEVEL*. I felt that somehow I was back in the land of the living, and as I continued to climb, the countryside became a little more hospitable. I pushed the little mare into a pleasant steady trot, but it was still uphill and I saw a hair tent beside a ruinous, nondescript building.

A break and some water for us both, I thought. As soon

as I stopped, I noticed that the tent was not so much a home but a tourist shop, selling Bedawi handicrafts. But the hospitality had not changed in two thousand years. It was the Inn of the Good Samaritan, and in a moment I was seated in the tent with tea and a bunch of grapes, while the little mare was given a brief drink outside. Again, an old man spoke of Glubb Pasha.

'If you see Abu Faris, remember me to him.' The old man was very, very old and so I did not tell him Abu Faris had been dead for some years. He would be happier to think his salaams had reached him.

Rested, I rode on and met the warden's wife and the matron at the next crossroads. They had come out with a packet of sandwiches and a welcome can of beer. I trotted on for another four hours until I reached the junction below the city. Both roads were confusingly signposted to Jerusalem, but there was no sign of the van. I dismounted and squatted on my heels beside the road for half an hour but there was still no sign of it, so I took the right fork and hoped for the best. The little mare was showing signs of weariness, so I dismounted and led her slowly up towards the Mount of Olives. The light was beginning to fade when a car pulled up beside me.

'Mr Nash, Mr Nash, I've found you!' It was the hospital handyman, who was on his way home after work. 'I will just go to a telephone to let the hospital know, and will return to show you the way. Just keep on up the hill.' Minutes later, the Reuters man appeared and asked me to remount for photographs; only just in time, as the light had now almost gone and as I paused and posed, my handyman guide returned and began to drive very slowly ahead of me.

I had always found that the end of a journey was totally anticlimactic and emptying. Thirty years earlier, I had arrived in Addis Ababa after seven months of travelling and found myself feeling physically sick, for no other reason than the release of tension. One minute one is involved in a struggle to get somewhere or do something, with a heightening tension as one approaches the objective, and then, flop – there is nothing at all. It was the same in South Yemen in those little wars: the intense excitement in, or expectation of a battle was followed by the same emotional vacuum. I expected it here and turned it over and over in my mind in those last couple of hours, leading the tired but gallant little mare the last few miles through the streets of Jerusalem. But it did not happen.

I arrived two hours after dark, still leading the pony, to find thirty or forty people standing on the steps of the hospital, clapping. I do not know what I expected to find, but I found it a little overwhelming and my instinctive first thought, born of the last eight months, for it was eight months almost to the day, was *What about the horse's water and fodder?*

Tony Morgan, the warden; his wife; and Pauline O'Donnell, the matron, led me to a flat that they had put at my disposal, where a chilled bottle of champagne awaited me, arranged by my two brothers through the Order in London. We drank a glass and they left me to go on to supper with Pauline when I had recovered a little, as the Morgans were out to dinner. I sank into a bath with a reloaded glass, revelling in the sybaritism of it, the champagne and the hot water easing the aches of that last thirty-mile day. An hour later a good supper, good company and physical tiredness combined to induce a contentment of spirit that flowed over me like a tide. It was all over – no more doubts, no more anxieties or frustrations; for better or for worse, it was done.

The next two days confirmed it: that immaculate hospital and its impeccable grounds, the patience and gentleness amidst horrifying political difficulties, the sheer dedication all confirmed it; however absurd or puny my contribution, it was worth it. When a Palestinian nurse, with twenty years of service there, shyly slipped an envelope containing a week's wages into my pocket as his gift to the hospital, I almost wept.

But outside, the prejudices and the anguish, the hatreds and despair so soured the taste, I was not sorry to leave Jerusalem. In that confined city, the shrines of the three faiths are more redolent of blood and bigotry than hope.

POSTCRIPT

This wasn't the last of James' fundraising adventures on behalf of the St John of Jerusalem Eye Hospital. In 2004, he undertook a pilgrimage to Santiago de Compostela accompanied by William, his horse and Matthew, his son.

James in his cart ready to set off – seen here with the St John cadets, William and Matthew